RENÉ LÉVESQUE

My Québec

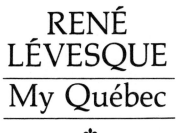

RENÉ LÉVESQUE

My Québec

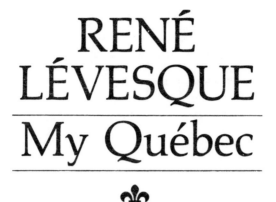

n METHUEN

Toronto New York London Sydney

English language edition for Canada
Copyright © 1979 Methuen Publications
A division of the Carswell Company Limited

All rights reserved. No part of this publication may be reproduced, stored in a retrieval system or transmitted in any form or by any means, electronic, mechanical, photocopying, recording or otherwise, without the prior written permission of Methuen Publications, 2330 Midland Avenue, Agincourt, Ontario.

English translation by Gaynor Fitzpatrick

© 1978 Editions Québec/Amérique, Montreal
English language rights reserved to Editions Québec/Amérique, Montreal

Original edition published in the French language under the title *La Passion du Québec* © 1978 Editions Stock, Paris.

Canadian Cataloguing in Publication Data
Lévesque, René, 1922-
  My Quebec

Translation of La passion du Québec.

ISBN 0-458-93980-3

1. Parti québécois. 2. Quebec (Province)—Politics and government—1960-   3. Quebec (Province)—History — Autonomy and independence movements. I. Title.

FC2925.2.L4813   329′.9714   C79-094136-8
F1053.2.L4813

Composition by
CompuScreen Typesetting Limited

Printed and bound in Canada by
T.H. Best Printing Company Limited

Contents

Publisher's Note

We wish to thank René Lévesque for his cooperation in the preparation of this English edition of *La Passion du Québec* and also J. Peter Meekison, editor of *Canadian Federalism: Myth or Reality,* 3rd edition, 1977, who acted as our editorial consultant and prepared the questions in the addendum for M. Lévesque's consideration. Mr. Meekison is currently Deputy Minister for Federal and Intergovernmental Affairs for the Province of Alberta.

The idea for the original volume was conceived by Claude Glayman, editor of the series *Les Grands Leaders Mondiaux* at *Editions Stock,* in Paris. The original interview was conducted by Jean-Robert Leslbaun, political advisor to *Le Nouvel Economiste* in Paris, France. His manuscript was modified slightly for the Quebec edition. This English language edition is a translation of the volume published in Quebec.

DECLARATION BY THE PRIME MINISTER OF QUEBEC BEFORE THE NATIONAL ASSEMBLY ON OCTOBER 10th, 1978

THE GOVERNMENT OF QUEBEC AND THE ROAD TO THE REFERENDUM

For the first time in our history, we, as Quebecers, will soon have the opportunity to decide for ourselves our political future.

This opportunity will not be ours immediately, but it is already dawning on the horizon. The Act setting up the machinery for the referendum was finally adopted just before we adjourned for the summer. Since we have committed ourselves to a referendum before the next elections, a new phase of our mandate has now begun, a phase in which we must define and explain the content of the referendum question. It is, therefore, time to bring this question up again and to confirm the essential elements.

We do so calmly and proudly, for we are sure that Quebec will not miss this historic opportunity to fully ensure its own freedom and its continued existence as a community.

This does not mean, however, that we are under-estimating the difficulties inherent in this phase nor the apprehensions which will surely be felt in many a mind. It is only natural that a number of people will still feel hesitant, uncertain, fearful of the changes such a decision may bring in its wake. If we leave aside, for the moment, the efforts of those who, in the future as in the past, will remain a dependent minority, the fact remains that a society cannot re-orient its whole existence without a certain amount of discomfort anymore than an individual can. Yet no nation can walk the path of its history without dealing with just such a situation, which is both one of its finest hours and a time of some anguish. And those who have the self-confidence and the maturity to accept this challenge as a step forward, whatever the problems that will follow, will never regret their decision.

Such should be our decision, and so it will be, as the course of history and our continued evolution demand it.

Maturity

As you know, the logical outcome we propose is called Sovereignty-Association. Our initial choice of a compound name was influenced by our desire to bring out the twofold objective of our constitutional position. We have no intention of first obtaining sovereignty and then negotiating an association. We do not want to end, but rather to radically transform, our union with the rest of Canada, so that, in the future, our relations will be based on full and complete equality. Sovereignty and association should therefore be attained concurrently without any rupture, once the people of Quebec have given us our mandate in the referendum.

Since the two concepts of sovereignty and association are so complementary that we have joined them with a hyphen, we must explain exactly what we mean by each of them.

Sovereignty is very simply, very naturally, for us as for any other people, the right to exercise full national responsibility. We are reaching our goal a little later than most, but no matter how many times we were delayed on the road, no matter how painful our progress, we never stopped moving stubbornly forward toward the day when we would be masters in our own house. From our distant colonial beginnings to our present half-fledged state allowed by the federal regime, we have constantly sought to rid ourselves of authority exercised from outside. Ever since the last century, when we won the partial sovereignty of a province, we have been demanding broader powers. Proof of this is found consistently in the stands taken by all those who, over the decades, have succeeded each other at the helm of Quebec government to administer a truncated version of sovereignty and often to defend their ship against threatened piracy. We too are doing the very same thing to the best of our ability, and will continue to do so as long as we remain within the existing system. But we do so knowing full well that in order to end once and for all the struggle of wills, the costly dividing up of energies and resources, the system must be replaced.

To achieve this end, the power to make laws and levy taxes must be exclusively ours. That is what sovereignty implies. Like any other nation, Quebec will be sovereign when its National Assembly is the only parliament able to legislate on its territory and when Quebecers pay only those taxes they themselves have decided to levy. For the first time in our history, our political tools and our principal financial and economic resources will be united in a single center where decisions will be made in the interests of the Quebec community.

Quebec's Relations with Canada

History, however, has taught us that such a legitimate affirmation by any people in no way precludes working together with other nations when this is mutually advantageous. Today, by reason of their close interdependence, the extent of their exchanges, and the facility of communication between them, nations are tending naturally to join forces in many fields to promote mutual development. We would certainly want to maintain close ties with Canada, since, for two hundred years, we have shared with our friends in the rest of Canada a common economic space, and many of our activities are closely interrelated and complementary.

We wish to keep intact this Canadian economic space which is as beneficial for us as for the others, with as few restrictions as possible on the traffic of products, capital and persons. To give a concrete example, there will be no question of setting up customs barriers or requiring passports for travel between Quebec and the rest of Canada.

And as a logical corollary to the preservation and good operation of existing markets, which we share, we also feel that together we must ensure that the currency used today is retained. Through negotiations carried out in good faith, it should be possible to entrust the management of currency and monetary policy to a joint central bank. Here again, we are taking this position in order to protect the existing economic space and to maintain the facility of commercial exchanges.

Working in this same spirit of both renewal and continuity, and ascribing to the concept of inter-dependence its full content of collective solidarity, Quebec will also have to take its place within the North American and North Atlantic alliances in order to contribute, however modestly, to the security of the Western democracies.

This is why, since the beginning, we have spoken of sovereignty and association as two complementary objectives which do not contradict each other, which follow the pattern of history and which also correspond better than any other formula to the development of nations. Carried along by the great political and economic currents now sweeping the world, Quebecers will even have the opportunity to contribute, along with the Canadian people, toward the development of this formula for the future, by defining their own brand of sovereignty-association.

At any rate, this much is clear: we can see nothing else which is likely to break the vicious circle, in which two different peoples are imprisoned, and deprived of what should go without saying: better understanding and respect for each other. And as people come to realize that our option is in no way founded on hostility, but that, on the contrary, it is intended to get us both out of an impasse which the present regime is incapable of solving; minds which were closed are gradually becoming more open, people are beginning to discuss the question and even official supporters of federalism feel compelled to take account of this, even if it is only to criticize, for their criticism is, to a certain extent, the hommage which the powerless pay to the politically prolific.

Step by Step

The government felt that it was important to clarify certain basic issues at this stage. For now the real debate begins on the solution which it intends eventually to submit to this Assembly, then to the people of Quebec and, finally, when we have been given a mandate through a referendum, to the whole of Canada, so that obsolete constitutional links may be replaced by an agreement which is permanent but at the same time flexible, and which can be adapted as required by changing conditions.

In closing, may we share some thoughts that we have had over the last few months regarding the steps to be taken that will lead us to our goal.

First of all, the government will continue to make public the technical studies it has had prepared on certain aspects of federalism as it exists today, on formulas for association which exist almost everywhere in the world and on economic exchanges between Quebec, the other provinces and certain countries. A study will soon be published on the role of the Supreme Court in the sharing of jurisdiction between the federal government and the provinces. Another study will follow soon, this one on the types of economic association which have already been tried in Europe and elsewhere.

In a few months, the government will also publish a more elaborate document on sovereignty-association. It will contain a more detailed description of those elements which appear to us essential to the smooth working of the formula, with respect both to those powers which will be exclusively Quebec's and to those which can be handled in common. Various possible options will be discussed regarding the final form which the planned association will take. These will include any additional joint undertakings which might be considered, the bodies which will see to the smooth running of the association, and so on. With the studies which will have come before, this government outline will mark the beginning of a period of intense national reflection, of exchanges and of dialogue between the government, the political parties and the general public.

Only after this period of consultation will the government submit a final question to the National Assembly, and ask that this question be put to the people by way of a referendum. Naturally, this question will be clear and precise, and it will relate to all aspects of the option which will have been defined collectively and which, subsequently, will require negotiation with the rest of Canada.

This process will take some time but will be completed before the end of the government's present mandate. The schedule involved will depend on the situation and there is no question of setting specific dates in advance for each step. The government will see to it, however, that discussion is carried on in the best possible conditions, without the issues being confused and without bull-dozing anyone. In this way, Quebecers will be able to contemplate their future calmly and be fully aware of what is involved, in a climate conducive to a fully democratic decision.

The many constitutional formulas, under which we have lived for 370 years, have always been more or less imposed on us from the outside and never freely ratified by all Quebecers. This time—at last—things will be different. For this reason, in closing, I call upon all groups and all political parties (including our own) to see to it that the forthcoming period of reflection is the least partisan possible, that it involves all the people and becomes truly their business. Only in this way can there be any assurance that the historic decision which we will then make will truly serve the interests of Quebec today and for generations to come.

PART 1

New Carlisle to Quebec

Monsieur Lévesque, would it be true to say that your origins and, subsequently, your professional experiences have been factors in determining your present political convictions?

Undoubtedly I came from a privileged background. My family lived in New Carlisle which is a small, anglophone village in the Gaspé with a population of about a thousand, most of whom were well known in the county and were descended either from the American loyalists or from British emigrants from Jersey and Guernsey. In New Carlisle and along the immediate coast the influence of the Robin, Jones and Whitman Company predominated. This company had been founded by an anglo-norman, Charles Robin, on a cod fishing monopoly and a chain of stores where the fisherman was obliged to purchase all his provisions. One had to travel four miles to the nearest francophone village, a village whose inhabitants worked in fishing, in agriculture or in the wood industry. I spent my youth in New Carlisle, except for a period in the Gaspé seminary after I had finished studying at the French School in New Carlisle, where there was constant conflict between bands of young French and English Canadians. We called each other names. They used to call us "pea-soupers"; we called them "craw-fish." In 1933 I entered the Gaspé seminary. For English Canadians, high school led to McGill University; for us French Canadians, school led nowhere. I was fourteen when my father died in 1936. My family was comfortably off, but only modestly so. We had a good library, along with an enormous intellectual curiosity which was my father's legacy to us. I had this intellectual curiosity right from the start and it has helped to assuage any feelings of inferiority I might have had. I had great admiration for my father. I learned English without being aware of it. I did not need to learn it in school, which is always so tedious a method, and I could soon speak it as well as French. I have therefore never felt any sense of trauma over language which could have influenced me subsequently, or given me the impression of having been treated unfairly on that account.

While I was in the seminary Quebec began its "quiet revolution." In 1934 Philippe Hamel's *Action Libérale nationale* put forward a restoration program, and the *Action catholique de la jeunesse canadienne*, with more than five thousand young members across the province, condemned the economic domination of foreign capital and the shackles imposed by the federal system. We were fairly well informed about this movement thanks to a system of rotating professors, who came from Montreal each year. In 1936 Maurice Duplessis finally reaped the harvest of the *Action Libérale nationale's* efforts. Immediately after taking office he made his first betrayal by declaring that he would not nationalize the power companies. There were other betrayals later. By 1937 my father had died. My mother left New Carlisle for Quebec in 1938. In the summer of 1938 I enrolled in Garnier college, which was run by the Jesuits, in Quebec. I wrote the following in the student paper: "Never forget that you are French Canadians, that your own people have been stagnating for generations, and that if they, the people, *your* people, do not act, they are lost!" In 1941 I received my bachelors degree after an erratic schooling in the arts faculty at Laval. Later, as a radio and subsequently a television journalist I travelled widely throughout the country. Each time I witnessed the diverging realities of our two societies I could not, through force of habit acquired young, suppress the thought that I was an integral part of a society, of a group, which was being stifled under the colonial system. When specific events led me to think about it, I realized that I did indeed feel colonized. But I was never personally influenced by it.

You have come a long way from New Carlisle. How would you describe the principal stages of your progress?

For the most part I moved instinctively. In the early 1940s I abandoned my law studies, or more correctly, they began to abandon me. My father had been a country lawyer and had dreamed that his oldest son would become one in turn. This did not entirely suit me. It was wartime, and like everyone of my age I felt this was the most important occurrence of the century, which would affect our whole lives. I was under threat of being conscripted into the Canadian army and, though I was willing to go overseas, I was not willing to go in the uniform of His Majesty. I therefore went to New York in 1943, and managed to join an information office, and then to be appointed war correspondent in the American Seventh Army. I went to war on a purely intuitive impulse. I did the same again at the beginning of the Korean war in the early '50s. I began in politics in 1960 in the provincial Liberal party, and was a minister in the Lesage government for six years. During this government's term of office the opening of the *Délégation Générale du Québec* in Paris sealed Quebec's official reconciliation with France, under General de Gaulle. The year following the Liberals' fall from power, 1966–67, was a year of reflection. I gave myself approximately eight years, more or less two legislative mandates, in politics, after which I would go back to journalism which had been my job after the war. This year of reflection, however, led my party and me to the resolution we still defend today, which is sovereignty for Quebec and a new form of association with Canada. Once we were convinced of the soundness of our purpose, a number of friends and other supporters persuaded me to step forward into politics again, since I was the best known among them.

What are the sources of your nationalism?

We had clashed with the federal government on several occasions and in several areas—social, fiscal and economic (especially on budgetary funding which has always been crucial to the federal system). This had enlightened me and led me to two conclusions, defended by the Parti Québécois, but whose origins go back to the 1930s when I was studying in college. Several of my professors, who were Jesuits, were already early nationalists and very closely linked to the *Action Libérale nationale,* which was the first organized group in Quebec to put forward a very distinct program for the renewal of the entity of Quebec. I now know that the nationalist germ—some would say "poison," others would call it a "fertile seed"—was implanted in those early days.

The long parenthesis of the war followed . . .

After the war I became a political journalist which, by Quebec standards, was almost an international career. My work took me from one political congress to another, to the United States, across Canada, and occasionally in the 1950s I reported from Europe and Korea. Being semi-rootless I inevitably made comparisons between what was happening in Quebec and other countries.

Slowly and at first subconsciously I became convinced that Quebec should safeguard its identity and develop into an independent political entity. In the mid 1950s an exceptional opportunity presented itself. As a radio journalist I had been solicited by television to produce an extraordinary program, the equivalent of which has never been seen in Canada, perhaps because it was subsequently considered to be too dangerous. The program was called "Point de Mire,"* which consisted of a study of one event or one problem occupying a central point in the news. With "Point de Mire" I was able to make the transition from international problems, in which I had become a specialist, to internal political problems, strikes, disagreements, questions of specific provincial or even federal character which were of consequence in Quebec. The program also helped to make me known, for at that time there was no exposure comparable to television. Subsequently, a very decisive event occurred: a strike was called at Radio Canada, which is where I worked. A large number of the station's employees were locked out by the management. The administration of Radio Canada fell under the federal jurisdiction, decisions or negotiations were made in Ottawa, and Ottawa was lying low. We therefore went in a delegation to Ottawa to request an audience with the minister responsible and the federal authorities, who gave us no reply for almost three months, though we knew well—and this was subsequently confirmed—that if the dispute had arisen on the English network of Radio-Canada, the matter would have been settled within two or three days. We had to wait sixty-eight days! I was scarred, even traumatized by that experience, so that sooner or later I felt I would have to enter politics.

At Radio-Canada you were part of the international service. You therefore gained experience in foreign affairs . . .

Especially after 1951 when I covered the Korean War as correspondent attached to a Canadian battalion which was part of the United Nations force sent to South Korea after the invasion by troops from the North. I got to know extreme poverty and the hostility of a whole nation. It was a brief experience but one which subsequently made me known as a lecturer. I was not really experienced in foreign affairs until 1953, when I was head of reporting services for radio and television. In October 1955 I followed Lester B. Pearson, then minister of External Affairs, on a visit to South East Asia during which he was supposed to go to Moscow to meet with Mr. Khrushchev. In fact the meeting took place in the Crimea and Khrushchev gave me the first interview ever given to a western journalist.

What were your war experiences?

Early in 1944 I embarked on a small boat, the *Indochinois*, which was docked in Halifax. In Halifax cargo convoys were formed which would return to England, escorted by destroyers. Despite the danger from German submarines our captain decided to go there alone, which gave us ten days of acute anxiety, especially during the night. At the age of twenty-one I therefore found myself in a very cosmopolitan London as the editor and announcer of messages to occupied France. I was confined to London for a long time, until February 1945, when I became attached to the Sixth Army Group and moved with the main body of troops, including the First French Army commanded by marshal de Lattre, east through France to the Rhineland, Bavaria and Austria.

Do you have any other war memories?

Yes, but I will save them for another time. Briefly, I followed the allied forces into Germany. I was present at the battle of Nuremberg, I was among the first to discover the horrors of Dachau, to find the well-treated prisoners in the Itter chateau, including Edouard Daladier, Léon Jouraux, Paul Reynaud and General Weygand. I saw Mussolini's body. I was one of the few journalists to hear Goering a few minutes after his surrender . . .

How did Quebec evolve during the period when you were a journalist?

M. Trudeau recorded accurately, in 1956, the malaise of the francophone community infiltrated by the English. He described French Canadians as a people who were defeated, occupied, decapitated, ousted from commerce, driven back from the towns, reduced little by little to a minority position, and diminished in influence in a country they had themselves discovered, explored and colonized. Despite the changes that had occurred in Quebec, it was still entertaining spiritual and cultural fantasies of a French Canada from one ocean to the other. Yesterday's nationalists were locked into economic conservatism. Let us not forget that in the late 1930s the nationalists looked for their deliverer to Mussolini, Salazar and De Valera, and that they preferred corporatist representation to democratic election.

Why did you offer yourself as a Liberal candidate in 1960?

In September 1959 Maurice Duplessis, leader of the Union Nationale which was successor to the Conservative party, died, exhausted by his term in power. He had been prime minister of Quebec since 1936 except for one interlude from 1939 to 1944. He was a lawyer of the old school whom no-one dared question. In response to the "defensive" and "negative" duplessist policies of provincial autonomy, the new provincial Liberal party, which had had its founding convention in 1955, offered a serious political program including free education, economic and social planning, a civil service commission, tight control of finances, an end to favoritism and to extortionate costs on public works contracts. Nothing particularly extraordinary, as you can see. It was necessary to make up for the time Quebec had lost, and the Quebec Liberal party was the only serious vehicle which could change things. This was the moment when the development of the province could open the way for a real awakening of the conscience of the whole Quebec people. Jean Lesage, the leader of the party and future Premier telephoned me: "If any of you want to come on board we can save you some constituencies." Four of us, Jean Marchand, Gérard Pelletier, Pierre Elliott Trudeau (who was the least well known) and I, were disgusted by the excesses of the Union Nationale, and opposed to the present, endless regime. However, when the time came for us to stand forward, I was the only one available. The three "doves" felt that they would be equally useful where they were. And then the thought of leaving their jobs . . .

They didn't want to make the leap. I selected the

constituency of Laurier. I was elected by a hairsbreadth with a majority of 129 votes, after a hard campaign in which I was severely attacked by my opponents. Nor did I spare them, a rabble of incompetent and doubtfully honest politicians who were "selling the country to foreigners," as the phrase went, and who at the same time kept it in a state of resigned under-development, and who restricted the right of association by bullying the unions, of which Quebec had great need, in order to maintain social peace. Concurrently, Ottawa saw John Diefenbaker's dull reign continue. Diefenbaker, a Conservative from the Prairies, had just refused an enquiry into the language problem, which was later set up by Lester Pearson, from Ontario, who knew just to what extent the future of his province was linked to that of Quebec. Pearson was elected in 1963 to head a minority Liberal government. He set up the Commission of Enquiry into Bilingualism and Biculturalism, whose preliminary report emphasized that Canada was going through the greatest crisis in its history.

Did the disappearance of Maurice Duplessis seem to you to mark the end of the long series of betrayals and setbacks in Quebec's history?

Yes. It was a deliverance to our generation which had been held back for so long by the Duplessis regime. It was imperative for Quebeckers to forget this stifling past and remember that very early in their history they had constituted a distinct people; that the little French colony with its 65,000 colonists, which was conquered in 1763 by a British Empire at the height of its powers, had in the past formed a distinct nation. For a century and a half, peasants and adventurers from France travelled across America, and those who put down roots by the lower Saint Lawrence developed a wholly different identity from France under the ancient regime. These people managed to survive, packed closely around their Catholic clergy and the land they owned. Atrociously poor, cut off from decision-making centers, deprived of cultural nourishment from their homeland, they remained productive, clinging obstinately to their own language and their land. This excluded them from urbanization, the establishment of manufacturing industries and the exploitation of natural resources, at first the exclusive field of the English, and subsequently of the growing anglophone minority, which was strengthened by the assimilation of immigrants. Quebec has never quite forgotten that it was once a potential nation. From time to time it has stirred: in 1880 when the English executed Louis Riel, the French-speaking leader of the prairie Métis; in 1917 over conscription, when the English supporting the Empire were in confrontation with the French isolationists; in the '20s and '30s as popular expectations were rising. The Second World War dealt a mortal blow to the old order. The need for change became permanent in the '50s, in a post-war period which brought unprecedented mobility, television and the consumer society. The population of Quebec doubled in twenty years. The program of the Union Nationale, in as far as it could be said still to have one, had not changed since 1931. Why did I make the move in 1960? Because it was necessary to do something to counter "duplessism." Things were simmering around me: as a journalist, in 1956, I had been present at the end of the campaign by Pierre Laporte, who was beaten as a liberal candidate; in 1958 Pierre Elliott Trudeau had tried to re-animate the *Rassemblement des forces démocratique;* the priests, Dion and O'Neil, published a book on electoral habits. Furthermore I had acquired a taste for participation in the political debates I had covered for Radio-Canada at the time of the American, Canadian and Quebec elections.

Why did you choose to enter politics through the Liberal party?

As I said before, it was the only viable opposition. In 1958, Jean Lesage, who had recently left federal politics, took over the leadership from Georges-Émile Lapalme, who, with his small group of parliamentarians, had tried to recruit to his cause a number of well-known persons. He had had no success. "Being a Liberal at this time is to burn one's bridges behind," he had concluded with some bitterness—the same man who later said: "Being a Liberal at that time was to be for social justice." Jean Lesage wanted to defend democracy against internal decay, and he proposed state control of the economy. For the first time we were dealing not with slogans, not with empty words, but with a written program, with written commitments. However it was not assured in 1958 that his call to "men of good will" would be heard. The death of Maurice Duplessis and, three months later, on January 2, 1960, that of his successor, Paul Sauvé, deprived the Union Nationale of leaders. The path to power was opening up in front of the Liberal party and Jean Lesage.

Were you immediately given a ministry?

The day after the elections Jean Lesage retired to consider the nomination of his ministers. There was a scramble for portfolios. Rumour had it that I would go to the new Department of Cultural Affairs. I really had not expected any appointment at all. When he called me, Lesage said the reason he was doing it was that I was almost the only person who had not asked for it! In fact I looked after Hydroelectric Resources and Public Works for one year (1960-61). Then I was given the new Ministry of Natural Resources (1961-1965). I was particularly interested in this problem because in the Gaspé I had heard a lot about the price of electricity! My ideas were clear: I wanted "to make every citizen of Quebec a shareholder in the exploitation of the immense national wealth of which Quebec is blessed." For the three years following our victory, the Liberal government did everything possible to reverse the trends adopted during fifteen to twenty years of negligence. As early as 1961 I declared: "French Canadians must use the state to pull themselves up from their position of servitude." While remaining loyal to the federal regime, I emphasized that the best way to achieve positive autonomy was to be sure to occupy those areas of authority accorded to the province of Quebec under the Canadian Constitution. After the second election in 1962 and the nationalization of the power companies into Hydro, the reform movement began to weaken, dulled by the routine of power and the subversive influence of the economic interests traditionally linked to the Liberals. However, nationalization was in no way a revolutionary idea. The hydro network was provincial property in both Ontario and Saskatchewan. The surprise was that, for the first time, Quebec was clearly indicating its will.

In the 1962 elections did you favor presenting the nationalization of hydroelectricity as an advantage for Quebec?

After two years of power the Lesage government needed new spirit. The Cabinet and several members of the party met at Lac-a-L'Épaule just north of Quebec City in September 1962. At this meeting Jean Lesage accepted the principle of nationalization, which enabled him to regain control of the members of the Cabinet, whose opinions often diverged. He made a shattering speech about the necessity to choose between the people of Quebec and the "trust."

Journalist Peter Desbarats[1] wrote about this later: "Everyone in the province knew what that meant. The 'trust' was Quebec shorthand for the financial center on St. James Street, the great houses along the Boulevard in Westmount," in a word all West Montreal's English establishment. "It meant afternoon tea . . . lunch at the Mount Stephen or one of the other clubs of the Montreal Anglostocracy. It was the kilted pipers skirling the customers out of Ogilvy's department store at the end of the day, the coming-out parties at the Ritz, and all those other comfortable and pleasant aspects of English life 1962. The 'people' referred to by Premier Lesage were French Canadians who clerked in the banks, and

---

Author of *René: A Canadian in search of a country.*

financial houses, who delivered the mail and laundry and milk in Westmount, sent their skimpy kids to the old schools among the tenements of east end Montreal and who talked hockey or politics all night." They were passive spectators, not the majority protagonists they could become.

Most Quebec politicians of your generation decided in 1965 to make their career in the federal Liberal party. Ottawa was then practicing a policy of opening up to francophones. Why did you remain in Quebec and in a career in provincial politics?

For the others it was basically a question of circumstances. In 1965, the men subsequently known as "the Three Wise Men" appeared: Jean Marchand, who has dedicated his life to union activity, and whom I had known since university; Gérard Pelletier, currently Canadian ambassador in Paris; and, ironically enough, the least convinced of the three, Pierre Elliott Trudeau, a professor of law at the University of Montreal, who was involved in the new federal socialist party, the NDP. I had met Jean Marchand, leader of the *Confédération des travailleurs Catholiques,* during the Radio-Canada strike. At that time I also met his colleague, Gérard Pelletier, who became the editor-in-chief of *La Presse* in 1961. The three of them headed together into federal politics because the time was right. I certainly wish to avoid any accusations of opportunism, but opportunity very often makes the thief. At that time Ottawa was looking for francophone ministers in order to create an illusion of *French power.* The door was open— they wouldn't even have to break it down! They were all about forty, ready for political activity—what followed confirmed this—and awaiting only an opportunity. To be fair, I think that none of the three felt the distinction between the federal and provincial level of politics as profoundly as I. Trudeau, in particular, has no particularly strong roots in the Quebec identity and culture. This is just a fact. He is half Scottish and anglophone through his mother, and French-

Quebecan through his father. Gérard Pelletier and Jean Marchand have never been conscious of federal/provincial differences. As far as they were concerned the two levels of government were natural complements . . . and they never saw any strong reason for making any changes.

I was the first of four—we were known as a group—to go into politics, in 1960. I remember a meeting I had, shortly before I made my decision, with one of the men I respect most among the federals, Stanley Knowles, who is probably close to being the doyen of the federal parliament. He had been there for ever, and at that time was one of the most active and committed members of the NDP, for which I could have had some inclination, like a brother of mine at whose place I met him one afternoon. Mr. Knowles suggested I make the federal "leap" into their ranks. It was at this exact moment that I knew that I would not feel at home there . . . perhaps because I knew Canada better than the others. As a journalist after the Second World War, I had crossed the country, from the Atlantic to the Pacific, more than twenty times. Events having taken me here and there, I had described every context of the country and, though there was as yet no political decision in my mind, I think that subconsciously, the more I got to know Canada the more I cut myself off from it. Every time I left Quebec for the other provinces—more frequently then than now—I had the impression of going into a foreign country, where my language was not understood, where my outlook and my way of working seemed "foreign." This is not to say that I was not well received. I have always been bilingual—I was almost born speaking English—but I felt myself in an alien context. Marchand, Pelletier and Trudeau did not have the same view, and their connection with the French language and culture did not colour their political concept of society. They were therefore able to make the federal choice very quickly. When it was suggested to me, I knew that I knew the country too well to be able to feel comfortable in a Cabinet which functions in English, which claims to represent my country but which, frankly, does not

give me the feeling that it assures the true representation of
Quebec's interests. I would never have felt at ease there, and
when Mr. Knowles made his suggestion I instinctively knew
this to be an irreversible fact. I knew that if ever I went into
politics it would be in Quebec, and not Ottawa. My former
friends, Jean Marchand, Gérard Pelletier and Pierre Elliott
Trudeau, chose the other path and were elected federal
members for Quebec in Ottawa in 1965. During the course of
their subsequent careers, Trudeau and Pelletier especially
have lost touch with their roots. I wonder whether they
themselves realize this. If so, they must sometimes wonder
whether the game justified the stake!

*The Liberal party lost the 1966 elections. The Union Nationale came into
power and Daniel Johnson put forward his "Equality or Independence"
formula. The issue was confused. How did Quebec politicians react?*

A few joined independentist movements, whose objectives
now seemed even less realizable than before. Of the Liberals
remaining in the party, some decided to go to Ottawa, like the
three companions I spoke of in our discussions of the years
1962-63. The federal Liberal party was in power. Others
remained members of the provincial Liberal party: they
returned to power in 1970 with Robert Bourassa. There was
political calm during the weeks in 1967 when Canada was
celebrating its one hundred years of federation, and guests
were arriving for the Montreal Expo.

De Gaulle's *"Vive le Québec libre!"* cry on July 24, 1967 was
the spark to the powder keg. The conservative wing of the
Liberal party which was terrified by separatism obstructed a
vote on a declaration of support for the General. I realized
that the party would never accept my theories. Even Robert
Bourassa, who had collaborated in the formulation of our
first declaration on sovereignty-association, no longer
wanted to support this stand—for monetary reasons, he said.

Despite this, you did not break with the Liberal party until 1967.

As minister for Family and Welfare (1965-66), I felt paralyzing pressures mounting. Initiatives for changes were harder and harder to get through. Social security, the telephone, immigration, each foray into these domains turned into a cul-de-sac. Also, I was very embarrassed—an understatement—by the existence of electoral funds, and by the provenance of these funds. On June 5, 1966, the Union Nationale, led by Daniel Johnson, carried the elections. The most surprising thing to us afterwards was to find the Liberal party's opposition so soft. It lacked direction. One group tried to reorganize the party. Wasted effort. At the 1967 congress we proposed sovereignty as an objective. I attempted to show that Quebec was an "under-developed, under-educated, colonial society, lacking in wealth and pride but, paradoxically, well nourished and comfortable, numbered by its elites and its "negro kings." It failed. Since we could not reform the party, we therefore decided to leave it. Those like Bourassa, who had worked with us until then, who have since tried to talk of federalism and have made renewed and progressive declarations of triumph over superficial, cosmetic reforms, have failed in turn.

You participated in the "quiet revolution" to a greater extent than any other minister in Lesage's government. How do you judge the revolution now?

"Quiet" gives us to understand that Quebec could not change radically. Nonetheless this same old Quebec, where a system of values had broken down, was trying to organize itself to face the modern world. Jean Lesage was a great Premier. He was very hard working, very nationalistic. He listened a lot. The government succeeded in nationalizing electricity very quickly, and in setting up an Economic Planning Committee. In 1964 the greater part of the government's effort was directed towards iron and steel, pension funds and Law 60 which created a Quebec Ministry of Education. From being one of the lowest, the investment budget in this sector became, and has remained, one of the highest (per capita)—with many errors on the way—but finally our human resources are developing. It was necessary to provide, at a given time, more or less equal opportunity for all.

In the economic sector the overall list of aims had to counter a well-implanted colonial system, the second-class status of the francophone majority, and a systematic remote control of major decisions by Ottawa and the head offices of foreign corporations. By 1966 Parliament had already passed laws on the *Caisse des dépôts et de placements*, a system of collective bargaining for workers in the public sector, and a public mining exploration company (SOQUEM). The brilliant success of the nationalization of hydroelectric power in 1962 was not repeated in other sectors, for example, the mines. In 1965, having been accused of being manipulated by the American Union of Metallurgists, I took a stand against the power of Noranda Mines, one of the largest Quebec companies: "The policy of Noranda Mines is to quash the workers by every means possible, infiltrating the unions, sabotaging collective bargaining and systematically refusing them claims which elsewhere were granted ten years ago."

In the end Jean Lesage enclosed himself in an almost Gaullian solitude, which was one of the reasons for his defeat. Another, more basic reason was certainly the fact that his government had not dared to define any specific directives on the national future. The "quiet revolution" was eventually nothing more than a mass of measures passed to suit the immediate circumstances, but which nonetheless served to dislodge Quebec from its passivity.

One has the impression that the reformist movement of this period ran out of steam. Why did Quebec fail to make the great leap on this occasion?

When the Ministry of Natural Resources, for which I was responsible, was created, they "forgot" to put the pulp and paper mills under its jurisdiction, despite the fact that the concessions granted to four giant companies amounted to 70 per cent of the forestry resources of the province. Everything I said or did was labelled "socialism." The most meagre achievements, the slightest suspicion of left-wing thinking drew attention. The influence of fifteen years of conservatism *à la Duplessis* was evident. I found myself sandwiched between traditional right-wing critics and voices from the new left, from the Quebec socialist groups. I was obliged to conclude that none of our projects for economic planning were making any progress. I lost many of my illusions while in the government. Like others before, the Liberal party fell into the trap of compromise between financial powers and political power. The enthusiasm we had generated subsided. When we came to power in 1960 we were not ready to put through reforms. We needed time to put the machine in motion, and this cost us essential momentum.

At what moment did you think of publicly questioning the federal regime and developing your Quebec alternative?

That was certainly in 1962 when I managed to convince the Liberal party to nationalize the private electricity companies in Quebec. This was done on May 1, 1963 when Hydro-Quebec took possession of the private companies for the sum of six hundred and four million dollars. I felt at that time that the nationalization of electricity, and increased access to education—the other major success of the Lesage government—were no more than tidying up measures whose effect would only be seen much later. Quebec still needed to define its major objectives and the means of achieving them. And this presupposed questioning federalism and moving towards sovereignty. As early as 1963 I said that Canada was made up of two nations, not ten provinces, adding that I felt like an Indian leaving his reserve each time I left Quebec. I contested the federal appropriation of credits for the national defense. I demanded that Quebec recover the direct taxes levied by Ottawa. I attacked "Confederation": "The current situation is abnormal. It is a jungle with a monster, the federal government, growing out of all proportion." By 1964 I was saying: "Quebec is stifling within the framework of an old, obsolete federation." I had a presentiment that Quebec would be "independent, and the free arbiter of its own destiny within the limits imposed by the interdependence of nations in the twentieth century." Others were dreaming of a different kind of federalism. The merry-go-round of slogans and deceptive nomenclatures, with which politicians are so extravagant, began. Claude Ryan confirmed in his editorials that he was resolutely federalist. Elected leader of the Liberals, he remained so and continued to try and square the circle with some kind of "new federalism." The young were particularly discontented.

On July 24, 1967, General de Gaulle made his famous "Vive le Québec libre!" cry from the balcony of Montreal's city hall. Was this a significant day for the independentist movements? To what extent do you owe to this declaration the fact that you are in power?

My choice was made public several months after General de Gaulle's visit, during the autumn of 1967. The Sovereignty-Association Movement was officially created between the end of October and the beginning of November 1967. Our decision was in fact already a longstanding one, as we had been talking about it since 1966. I recall that one of us, a Liberal member of Parliament called Francis Aquin, who is no longer in politics, was much more keen than us to cement close relations with Europe. I think that his student background and his reading had very profoundly imbued him with a great attraction for European culture, and immediately following de Gaulle's *"Vive le Québec libre!"* he decided to embrace the idea of a total break with Canada, and to make an official declaration to this effect. Shortly afterwards he became the first separatist member of Parliament.

As we were all still to be Liberals for several months, and even though we didn't adopt the Liberal party's churlish attitude towards de Gaulle, we tried right up to the last moment to convince Aquin to give up his declaration. He held fast and decided to move as a lone warrior. He was soon dubbed a "gaullist" member. This was precisely what we had wanted to avoid for the movement which by now we had been planning for more than a year. And it is one of the major reasons which made us delay its creation as its intent was in fact in the direction of the General's cry. I do not wish to belittle the impact of de Gaulle's declaration. On the contrary we owe him enormous recognition for having made us known throughout the world with this fortunate blunder. However, it was just as essential that our decision not appear to have been moved forward, as it was for us to shackle our colonial and "follower" reflexes.

In the midst of the confusion on that summer day, what were your impressions?

After the balcony incident, which everyone still talks about today, I mixed with the crowd in order to get to where I had left my car, not far from the city hall. On the way I came across a group of very happy, excited youths who were chanting: *"Québec libre! Oui, oui, oui! de Gaulle l'a dit! Oui, oui, oui!"* This convinced me very firmly that we had to take very great care and not jump onto de Gaulle's bandwagon, with all its accompanying risks of appearing to be replicas of the man.

After de Gaulle left power, and with even greater reason after his death, we tried as much as possible to emphasize not only the historic importance, but also his very concrete and very precise perception of the Quebec situation. On his return to France he tried to explain his words. I remember that we went through all his speeches with a fine toothcomb but I never found anything in them that could ever be construed as meddling or a distortion of the truth. I was sorry to read later that the incident had brought a lot of negative reaction to the General. To a number of left-wing groups in France, who had never put much time into investigating the exact situation in our country, it appeared that the Quebec problem was his own invention.

In 1967 you left the Liberal party to set up your own party. Ten years later you became Premier. What happened in between?

Barely a month and a half after my resignation, several friends and I had gathered together a group of several hundred people and decided that before the end of 1967 we would form the Sovereignty-Association Movement, which was something of a temporary domicile. We were able to regroup men who were already going in the same direction, and notably the *Rassemblement pour L'indépendance nationale* (RIN) headed by Bourgault and d'Allemagne. This happened in 1968 when we drew up the constitution of the Parti Québécois. Since then there have always been diverse tendencies manifest within the party: the "hardliners" who are the offspring of the RIN; the evolutionists who are those of the Sovereignty-Association Movement; and then those who put the social before the national, and vice versa. But the people of all these opinions consider that change will be brought about by the growing awareness of Quebecers themselves, with respect for our institutions and without recourse to violence. Violence is specifically condemned, *vide* the restraining of the Quebec Liberation Front terrorists, whose ideology was a desperate mixture of anarcho-nationalism and kindergarten marxism. Since 1968 the P.Q. has succeeded in uniting almost all currents of independentist thinking around the idea of sovereignty-association. It has become a large, popular party whose funds are raised by voluntary contributions from its members. At the same time the long march began, its regular process was being regularly disguised by the distortions caused by our ballot system: 1970, 7 seats;

1973, 6 seats; and then the tidal wave of 1976, with 71 seats. In fact the idea of an "independentist" party, which would at the same time be moving towards a Scandinavian-type social democracy (which is the maximum "progressivism" possible for a serious left-wing group in the North American context), was a response to long and deeply felt desires and aspirations. I think that we are proof of this.

You have been in politics for seventeen years. This has apparently not changed the modest way in which you live.

I have never had extravagant tastes. After the Liberal party's defeat in 1966, which they asked for through having no concept of the logical follow-up of their first successes, I could have acquired material success in administration, teaching or some federal position. I preferred to participate in the founding of our party and live on my parliamentary salary and, when I was defeated, on my pension and my journalistic articles. But rest assured, I eat three meals a day, and have the time and the means to take a holiday at least once a year. More often when I can. And I also manage to find some free time to see a certain number of friends, the closest of whom are naturally from among the *"péquistes."* We have worked together for so many years, and our shared confidences have brought us closer and created links between us. However, a certain number of my friends do not share my opinions. This does not stop me seeing them with a very special pleasure, because I like meeting with a sort of opposition, and have invigorating arguments, which quite frequently leads us into "quarrels."

One could add to the seventeen years in politics the years I spent working in television, i.e., the years from the mid-fifties onwards, since this earlier career gave me all the characteristics of a public figure obliged, even in this environment, to protect his personal life.

So, one thing leading to another, and I am still here,

and as long as people want me, I shall continue. I am "employed" to the full, and I think this is essential. There is no other job which demands as much of, and sometimes beyond, one's capacity for what one can reasonably be expected to have by way of experience and judgment. Power is perhaps exactly this very intense feeling of functioning as if one were incapable of doing anything else. In this sense only, power has turned my head!

Rumors have circulated about the state of your health, and also about a plot against you. This is one way of approaching the subject of your successor.

One can eliminate the plot immediately. This kind of rumor will persist as long as there is speculation about the political future of Quebec. There are some circles, which can be easily identified, in whose interest it clearly is to try to destabilize Quebec and its government, or its economy, because this is the normal reaction of a colonialist center to a colony. It is normal, even predictable, that these circles will try to generate panics, until the "colony" is emancipated. Assassination attempts, plots . . . they are the risks of the job. Society everywhere is being exposed to an increasing number of disquieting violent episodes, the victims of which are not only politicians. This resurgence of violence indicates that something is becoming sterile in our values.

As far as my health is concerned, I am one of those people of whom one says that they look ill, although they have an iron constitution. I often look fragile, and even a little worn. This has gone on for twenty years and I have never been really sick.

As for my eventual successor, I can assure you that there will be no problem. It is enough to look into the party's growth and see that it now has branches almost everywhere. The Parti Québécois has recruited many of the most advanced people in Quebec, the new elites, the most notable leaders of the thirty-to-forty-five generation. Some of them, some of the best of them, are already in the provincial Cabinet, or in Parliament. A succession problem will only present itself in terms of an overexcess of riches from which to make a selection.

What were the consequences of the October 1970 crisis?

First, it affected the reputations as defenders of individual liberty that Trudeau especially, and Bourassa at the provincial level, boasted. The so-called "liberal" government of Quebec accepted a wave of more than four hundred and fifty arrests and more than three thousand searches without warrant. At least four hundred of the people arrested were finally released without any charges being laid, but they had spent several days in prison, had been searched, photographed and were not allowed to communicate with parents or lawyers. This crisis, however, concealed another, more hidden one. Francophone Quebecers were becoming a marginal society, even in Quebec. The French language could not be used in big businesses. Barely 10 per cent of new immigrants entered French schools. Francophones had the lowest incomes. And finally, the provincial government emerged from this crisis even weaker in respect to Ottawa. The federal government appeared the stronger of the two. Quebec was finding out that it had real power.

PART 2

❃

The Experience of Power

On November 15, 1976, by giving it 41 per cent of the popular vote, Quebecers assured the victory of the Parti Québécois. In your first speech you stated very emotionally: "I have never been as proud as I am tonight of being a Quebecer." However, you are allowing time to elapse between this victory and the referendum which will decide on the independence of Quebec.

Yes, but on November 15, 1976, Quebecers had the courage to make the decisive step. By conferring government office on the *péquistes* instead of the Liberals, they conquered a fear of two centuries standing. Quebec was first a French colony, then a British colony, and finally a colonized province. Quebec has never made its own decisions. Even in the very recent past, the governing of Quebecers was decided elsewhere, less in Quebec than in Ottawa, or even in Montreal in some circles. All the efforts we have made during the last two years have been directed towards one objective: controlling our own affairs. We will start with sufficient control of our economic life which, alone, can ensure the survival and development of our language and our national identity.

How did the take-over of power from Robert Bourassa go?

Fairly comfortably. At first, naturally, we were a little strained, a little gauche, especially in front of the battery of cameras and the crowd of journalists who insist on being present at this kind of event. Later we went out for lunch together, which is traditional. Without going into too much detail, Robert Bourassa gave me a sort of briefing on a number of points, but it was in a slightly bitter fashion, which is understandable in the light of various incidents during his electoral campaign, which had been very difficult both for him and his entourage. The Quebecers accused Robert Bourassa's government of having worsened relations with the union movement in 1976, during the course of a series of strikes in the public services in the province. In addition, every time they stepped forward they met with accusations of corruption, and the "imprudence" of certain people close to the center of power. Bill 22, which was claimed to resolve the language problem, especially in the schools, had succeeded only in tearing Quebec apart, dividing the anglophone supporters of the Liberal party. On the day when power was handed over, we discussed the time necessary for him and his government to vacate the offices. We discussed when we could become operational. We discussed the economic situation, the budget, and several of the most urgent problems which we were shortly to inherit. In sum we were, more than anything else, relaxed, and relieved.

In your view, what were the principal factors which, along with the fall of the Bourassa government and the spectacular about turn of public opinion, determined your party's ascent to power?

At least three-quarters of a government's responsibility for defeat is its own. Whatever the factors which led the electorate to change teams it also is evident that the feeling of "new faces" and "making a clean sweep" played a part. When this happens, nothing can be done. . . . It was particularly painful for Bourassa and his entourage, as there was a complete breakdown of contact with the electorate which he seems not to have perceived. Perhaps this was one of the after effects of the October 1970 crisis. The government, its leader, and the Minister of Justice shut themselves off in an unprecedented manner in a state of isolation, which was accentuated by the system of security and dictated, I suppose, by circumstance. It then became a more or less permanent habit to be isolated, to be protected behind security barricades. When we took power we had to shake off the police apparatus and open the door wide. At that time the seat of government which is, and must remain, public resembled in essence a fortress. This breakdown between the people and the government without any doubt explains some of Robert Bourassa's political and economic failures. It is said that power corrupts. The Liberal government had been in power for six years. The party I had started in had tried to reform itself during the calm period of the "quiet revolution" in the '60s. It had even achieved some major reforms; but after this awakening period of the '60s, when Bourassa gained power in 1970 he brought into his team a lot of the rejects from the Lesage government. Let us just say that very few rigorous reformers were appointed to Bourassa's entourage. In the course of six years the government became weak, almost to the point of disintegration during its last year. This decay even touched the administration. A sort of laxity pervaded the large departments and state bureaucracy. Scandals erupted, others were lying around. There was flagrant collusion between the state and the interest groups.

The opposition emphasizes that you were elected less on a "sovereignty" platform than on a platform of economic and political reform. Bourassa's team was unpopular. Could the Quebecers have elected you simply in order to overthrow this team?

The Parti Québécois' opponents will not succeed in stealing from us the victory we won on November 15, 1976. Before the ballot they continually warned Quebec against what they called the apocalyptic consequences for Canadian unity of a *"péquiste,"* i.e., separatist vote. The electors did not listen to these Cassandras. There is therefore some dishonesty in trying to diminish the importance of the ballot on November 15, 1976. The more so because this victory is now inscribed in the "long march" of the nationalists. Let us not talk here about the twentieth century, about Papineau's revolt, or that of Lower Canada in 1837. Since the 1940s every election in Quebec has been carried on "nationalist programs": the "Popular Bloc" of the war years, M. Duplessis' jingoistic nationalism, Lesage's "Masters in our Own Home", Daniel Johnson's "Equality or Independence." For the last twelve years the supporters of sovereignty have made steady progress. What was deceiving was the number of seats held in the National Assembly: in 1970, the Parti Québécois won 23 per cent of the vote but only 7 seats; in 1973 it occupied only 6, but won 30 per cent of the vote which represents one francophone out of two. The November 15, 1976 victory was a natural conclusion. It was also a beginning. The enthusiasm which spread on election night, the feeling of pride which came over every Canadian francophone, every Quebecer, *péquiste* or non-*péquiste*, and over threatened minorities in other provinces show that the movement is irreversible. Quebec had swung around. A consciousness had appeared which will not be dulled. November 15, 1976 was a point of no return.

What legacies did you find when you took office?

Firstly, a very tight economic situation. We are still living with the very painful after effects of the orgy of spending which accompanied the Olympic Games. That, and other weaknesses had led Quebec and its population of six million to the position of being one of the largest borrowers on the international market. The rhythm, the cadence of borrowing had passed from 6 per cent a few years previously, to 12 per cent of the gross national product. Twelve per cent was excessive and the rate had to be reduced. We also had to reintroduce order to the budgetary operation as a whole.

The government was sworn in at the end of November, 1976. Early in December almost in a panic, we urgently called a special session of the National Assembly on account of a number of emergencies which had to be met December 31.

We took the first step in our house cleaning somewhat sorrowfully, imposing on the administration of the city of

Montreal, which did not want to accept it, some $200,000,000 in new taxes spread, obviously, over several years. These taxes were to cover the $200,000,000 in "Olympic debts" which the city had contracted and the burden of which, for its own reputation, it was absolutely essential to require it to assume. From the moment a country addresses foreign markets regularly for loans, its credibility or "credit rating," so-called, must be sound. Jacques Parizeau did not mince his words in his 1977 budget speech. We have been obliged to retrench, to tighten ministerial belts in almost every sector. As a result of this courageous policy the most respected American financial circles have granted credit to Quebec and to Hydro-Quebec. We are all the more satisfied with this first stage of reorganization, since dark suspicions had been stirred up by some of our opponents. They tried to parody us, and indeed are still trying to depict us under the guise of adventurers who don't know how to do their sums. It was therefore even more important to prove that we did know, and our operation succeeded. The placement of government of Quebec or Hydro-Quebec loans in Germany, in Switzerland, on the Eurodollar market, and in the United States, has served in part to adjust our image as a serious country—and image counts for a lot in those circles—and progressively to prove the health of Quebec's financial operations.

Do you think that the repatriation and rewriting of the Constitution as proposed by the Trudeau government will serve to Quebec's advantage?

If the referendum is decisive, as we hope it will be, the federal Constitution which is of British origin, will become a museum piece. We therefore consider profoundly insufficient the recent proposals put forward in June 1978 by Mr. Pierre Elliott Trudeau aimed at the "repatriation" and rewriting of the Constitution. These are old questions that many federal-provincial conferences have not succeeded in resolving ... because the provinces fear they will lose those guarantees of autonomy assured them by the British North

America Act, but gnawed at by Ottawa. The constant failure of these periodic endeavors is related in particular to a fundamental contradiction which has existed since the beginning: between the French people in Quebec who need autonomy, more and more self government, and the anglo-Canadian people who would easily be able to accommodate a more and more centralized regime because they are the ones who would control it.

Since November 15, 1976, official optimism is de rigueur. However nothing has definitely been won. Have you ever been tormented by fear of failure?

I go to bed, I sleep, I wake with the feeling of urgency. The relative weight of Quebec, because of its diminishing birth rate and its low rate of immigration, compared with Ontario especially, is decreasing continually, from one census to another, within the Canadian entity. In consequence the socioeconomic weight of the country is also declining in relation to the more rapid development occurring in the west of Canada. But the feeling of urgency springs from something else. The Parti Québécois is the heir to various movements, more or less organized, which date back to around the '30s. These were small groups, "voices in the desert," which preached emancipation, did their tour of the circuit and disappeared. During the '60s, organized groups which presented candidates appeared. The Parti Québécois, created ten years ago, demanding unimaginable effort, expenditure of energy and devotion, was the end result of this series of stages. The idea of emancipation literally got to the guts of the people defending it. If everything fell through or were simply delayed, it would be very difficult to recharge the batteries, renew the energy, and to start another movement, or even to ensure the survival of the current movement after the long period of depression which would follow a setback in the will for emancipation.

In financial circles, the speech you made in January 1977 at the Economic Club in New York has been considered as both imprudent and fearless . . .

Of course! Having taken office the Parti Québécois should, according to our professional Cassandras, have avoided approaching two subjects: its "socio-democratic" program and its independentist objectives. Confidence both in Quebec's credit worthiness and its economy could have been bought for the price of silence. I chose to speak. I was able to give all the assurances necessary to those who might have thought that Quebec was heading for, to some extent, a "Cuban" experience. Many of the Parti Québécois' programs are related, more or less, to similar proposals put forward in other provinces or at the federal level. Why should Quebec's wish to intervene in the asbestos industry be considered a dangerous attitude? Ottawa acted in the same way in the reorganization of the aeronautical industry, and the creation of Petro-Canada. Saskatchewan did the same in the potash industry. And the progress made by our government on the question of automobile insurance is not so revolutionary within the present Canadian context.

We are told that it would have been easy to reduce the gap between the price of Government of Quebec bonds and Government of Ontario bonds if we had agreed to remain silent about these rather difficult political questions.

Unfortunately many people have not examined what happens on the financial market closely enough. Every time there is a change of government in Quebec, the price of Government of Quebec bonds drops for several months, at least in Canada. But in fact the greatest differences between the price of government bonds in Ontario and Quebec did not occur following the victory of the Parti Québécois. It happened, curiously, in the months following the Bourassa governments succession to power in 1970. And what could be more "orthodox" than that government?

Was the political uncertitude provoked by the accession to power of the Parti Québécois one of the causes of economic decelleration?

Many anglophones and some members of the business world were certainly worried, or even panicky, about the accession to power of an independent, "socio-democratic" party. But in the confusion of true and false rumors that we know circulate it is difficult to differentiate between what concerns the state of the economy and what concerns the pursuit of a long and tenacious option to change the society and political organization of Quebec. It is true that 91 so-called head offices were transferred out of Quebec in the atmosphere of artificial panic at the beginning. But 79 of them did not even have their telephone numbers listed in the Montreal directory! It was madness. Jacques Parizeau said as much in his 1978-79 budget speech: "Denouncing a minimum wage of $3.00 when, under the previous government, $2.87 was acceptable is mere symbolism and childishness. Making an issue out of Bill 101 regulations applicable to head offices, and for which the law specifically makes exceptions, and raising a fuss even before they are published, is politics in its most traditional sense. . . . The referendum will have very little influence on the price of copper in London. And it was certainly not the debate on national unity which caused the building of too many hotels in the center of Montreal. The most I can acknowledge is that political discussions in Quebec are responsible for several thousand houses in the west of the metropolis going on the market; and that that has affected the volume of new construction in 1977.

Canadian life is punctuated by rivalry and confrontations between the federal and the provincial levels of government. How important was the role played by Ottawa in your accession to power?

Let us consider our position in 1976. The provincial government then had limited resources at its disposal for the fulfilment of its priorities. Quebecers were already carrying a very high fiscal burden in relation to the other provinces. On the other hand the federal government, in addition to its other powers, especially in the areas of monetary and fiscal policy, had, and still has, at its disposal much greater economic freedom to manoeuver in its interventions. It is not content with those sectors normally reserved for Ottawa by the Constitution but, more and more frequently during Trudeau's ten years in office, has shamelessly encroached on areas which fall under provincial jurisdiction. Because of its unlimited spending power, because of the degree of blackmail which this allows it to exercise, the federal government has therefore managed to direct the economic and social organization of Canada. This situation is particularly serious for Quebec which is carrying the heaviest costs because, since the "quiet revolution," it has also been supporting programs of its own.

Yet Quebec is not impoverished. It controls half the fiscal resources raised within its territory.

More or less. But the more significant portion, that which has the greatest effect on development, remains in federal hands. This does not effectively alter the fact that Quebec controls a sizeable fiscal portion, though it can be used in fewer ways than in Ottawa. We also have a sort of "secular arm" in state corporations, which we have not yet learned to operate with the greatest desirable efficiency. They enjoy a large degree of administrative autonomy, and therefore sometimes develop plans which are lacking in liaison with the plans of their sister organizations. This has to be corrected. A purchasing policy more systematically directed towards Quebec goods and services would permit us both to consolidate and modernize our industry, and to create new sectors, mainly in manufacturing. Less than 3 per cent of the asbestos fiber extracted in Quebec generates further manufacturing operations. It has been calculated that if 20 per cent of the fiber was processed in Quebec we would create almost 8,000 jobs, in other words we would more than double the number of jobs existing now mostly in the mining area. This would not be inconsiderable, since in 1977 we lost 29,000 jobs in the soft sectors of our industry, which were threatened by increasing imports, and which exceptional protective measures were able to protect only slightly towards the end of the year. Did you know that at one time the purchasing officers for the official car fleet had to conform to ground rules which forbade the purchase of Renault cars coming out of a Quebec plant in which the government was the principal shareholder! A simple illustration of a polito-economic muddle which is a legacy of an over-lengthy tradition of dependence, and equally of the irresponsibility with which Quebec has long been familiar.

You have often claimed that Quebec carries a "triple crown" consisting of increasing indebtedness, excessive taxation and chronic unemployment.

Well, in less than two years our debts have been reduced, and our financing needs in 1977 represented only 9 per cent of provincial revenues, compared with 14 per cent in Ontario, and 25 per cent in Ottawa. In 1977 we did nothing to reduce the Quebecers' tax burden. Instead we reduced taxes on corporations, which is somewhat unusual for social-democrats, but which was dictated by very deep concern for economic growth. However, in the 1978 budget we were able to introduce several reductions in taxation in favor of individual taxpayers, to the extent of $300,000,000 in 1978 and $500,000,000 in 1979. Our achievements are less evident in unemployment, since we do not control the real economic levers which remain in the federal domain. On the other hand Quebec continues to enjoy a credit which those who cry catastrophe have not managed to impair, despite increasing unemployment. The day Quebecers are masters of their own resources and their own economy we will be able to make further progress forward.

What are your medium-term plans for economic and social reform?

It is inconceivable that we can make reforms within a few months that others failed to make in ten years of effort. This does not mean that we refuse to speed up certain processes, drawing on the evolutionary experiences of those societies which serve as our models. But we can certainly not instantly lay a veneer of foreign solutions on our society, which would be to risk almost immediate failure. When we discuss industrialized societies with a high standard of living, or consumer societies, we find ourselves perforce facing analogous, sometimes even identical problems. Foreign models are useful and can give us inspiration. But once again we have to take into account the pace at which reforms were introduced elsewhere to achieve these results. In conclusion, there are certain innovations which we wish to adapt and introduce in pace with the rhythm and capacity for absorption of Quebec society.

Despite your popularity, there are some circles in Quebec which expect to see their society transformed and are already criticising your prudence and complaining that the reforms are taking a long time to come.

Gérard Pelletier, who is a friend, but also an adversary on the political level, has already said in a sort of political half-testament he made during a press conference before he left for Paris: "Quebec is becoming ungovernable!" I do not share his pessimism.

Let us go back fifteen years. The slogan "the quiet revolution" had been adopted. The adjective "quiet" was used to reassure, because no revolution is truly quiet. But already by 1960 it was a revolution in the real sense of the word which implies a fundamental change. It happened quickly in Quebec and it has had a deep impact. Our rural and clerical society literally erupted. Since the end of the Second World War it had been simmering, and finally the covers which had been holding down the steam for too long flew off. It is obvious that a society which, in less than a generation, completely changed course under the strong evolutionary currents of our times, is a society whose prospects are unstable. The pessimist concludes that this society is ungovernable. The optimist—as is my case—who believes in the force of the will, also thinks that men, providing they know what they want, can direct their own history; he feels that he can count on the extraordinary potential generated in the new spirit and rebirth of Quebec.

Some people in Quebec are whispering that your government is not committing itself enough and that this is evidence of political opportunism.

The referendum is, for us, a fundamental objective. We must put as much luck as possible on our side in order to ensure victory. Let us hypothesize that the referendum will take place in two years. How many essential questions can we concern ourselves with within a two-year cycle? We must try to resolve the maximum number before the referendum, because certain questions cannot be left to drag on indefinitely. But how do we deal with these questions in a way that will not hamper our chances in each key sector at the time of the referendum? Consider the question of education. There are many weak spots and certainly changes will have to be introduced. We published a green paper in which we proposed a certain number of reforms. Knowing full well that discussions could spin out throughout this three-year cycle, we have to establish a timetable for those reforms which seem the most urgently called for. But we also have to take into account that the referendum will fall due, and think of the capacity of Quebec society to absorb priority reforms. It is not easy to work as social-democrats, good administrators and reformists in many sectors without risking compromising the central issue—a democratic decision on our future.

Do you not fear that, as often happens in politics, you will be worn out by your first months in power and unable to keep up the pace of reform?

For a new government which arrives, as was our case at the end of November 1976, with only one person who has had any experience of power, the most important task is to give a rapid apprenticeship. The first year is necessarily a year of running in and fulfilling pledges. It was with this in mind we insisted that the quantity of our electoral pledges be extremely limited, and that each of these be clearly defined. If I remember correctly, there were nine.

Our first priority, one which has never been achieved in any so-called democratic society, was to eliminate the relationship between money and politics, i.e., to open the so-called "party coffers" which have always been shrouded in secrecy. We decided, in order to abolish the concealed power in the funds, to vote a Bill which would oblige each party to disclose each year, and under oath, its sources of income, which should be verifiable. It was understood that the parties would in return receive extra financing from the state for secretarial and organizational operations. We believe that the parties should be maintained essentially by individual citizens. This is one of our fundamental principles. If members of a trade union or shareholders in a company wish to contribute they can always do so, but on an individual basis, as individual citizens.

Another obligation that was dear to me: I wanted to initiate quickly a more "civilized" policy towards senior citizens. After long discussions we decided purely and simply that medication would be supplied free to all persons aged sixty-five and over.

We had also undertaken to begin to reform automobile insurance. This has been done.

We knew that this period of apprenticeship would be very difficult. We chose to spotlight our pledges by reducing them in number, and we systematically realized them as well as possible during the first few months. This gave us our initial experience while protecting us with guardrails. We could not spread ourselves in all directions. This did not, however, prevent us from starting to gather other information on matters which concerned us, notably in the economic and industrial areas.

The economic situation in Quebec is difficult. In which sectors do you anticipate economic growth?

It took us only ten months to understand all our economic weaknesses. The previous government worked predominantly on appearances. By this I mean that for many years there had been an enormous amount of negligence in essential sectors, notably on large, spectacular projects such as the Olympic Games. They had adopted the practice of making frequent calls on foreign capitals to replace the private or public initiatives of Quebecers. Drawing up an economic policy is something else however! It takes time. It is laborious. One must make calculations, evaluate the risks. During the first year we managed to prepare all the information we required. Within the limits of provincial jurisdiction we have proposed all the section headings for what could constitute an economic policy for Quebec until we have obtained the more complete and more autonomous means necessary to achieve a national economic policy. The most disturbing areas, those we call our "soft sectors," are legacies from the beginning of the century. These sectors were weakened by a completely insane federal importation policy. In order to sell Canadian products, such as wheat from the west, we sacrificed jobs in textiles, furniture, shoes and clothing. These sectors of the Quebec economy cannot compete against the low-income countries. I have nothing against western grain. All the better if they manage to sell it, but not at our expense. It is Quebec that regularly suffers the loss of jobs corresponding with this bargaining which is done behind our backs. We intend to help those among those industries that can remain profitable to rationalize their operation, and little by little to reorient the young members of our work force who can be recycled into other sectors. This requires a certain amount of time. We need to conduct a concentrated offensive on Ottawa in order for the federal government to turn to several emergency regulations which exist, but which are never applied, in order to ensure three or five years' temporary protection for our industries. They will thus have their opportunity to rationalize and convert.

Within the present context we are obliged to wait for intervention from Ottawa. The federal government holds the reins. In the textile and clothing industry, if I am not mistaken, in comparison with such major importing countries as the United States, England and the Common Market, Canada has allowed itself to become the most impoverished through tolerating importation beyond all economic sense. With its immense market of 220,000,000 people, America imports no more than one fifth of what Canada allows! And since the fact is that more than half the Canadian jobs in this section have been situated in Quebec for more than fifty years, it is consequently Quebec which loses more jobs than any other province. This is evidence of Ottawa's lack of concern and one of the signs of the inconsistency and failure of its economic policy: the resignation of the federal finance minister, lowering of the dollar on the international markets, unprecedented budgetary deficits; incurable "stagflation".... The list goes on and on. . . .

To what do you attribute the persistance of unemployment, given that businesses are receiving more aid than individuals?

I don't think that is true. In any case one must admit that the social security system and income protection, which are assured by both federal and provincial measures, have almost reached their limit. It would perhaps be better to do something other than continually increase the expensive measures provided by the social security system. It would perhaps be more desirable to move in the direction of greater selectivity, to find out the areas of real need, what correctives can be applied to safeguard the incentive to work, one being a formula for a minimum guaranteed income. Otherwise we will finish by being a socially indolent society, and there are certain worrying signs pointing in that direction.

Business does not receive support, especially at a time when the markets are increasingly unsettled. But this is a necessary policy practiced by every country in order to save jobs. The idea is not to protect shareholders; nonetheless, since they are there, naturally they benefit. The first thing which concerns us when we hear of the impending collapse of a business is to find out how many people will be out on the streets as a result. However, there is a limit to the number of industrial lame ducks we can support.

We can no more support every business in difficulty than we can let them fail indiscriminately, which could seriously damage the social fabric of the country, especially in the case of small towns, communities and relatively isolated groups of people. There are always uncomfortable choices to be made when the times are difficult, and the times are not particularly good just now. It is true that the current level of unemployment is unacceptable. If this level were to increase or simply to be maintained, it would, quite simply, become shameful. It is the result of the structural weakness of our economy. It is even more the result of the badly thought out and increasingly catastrophic policies of the federal government which, from an economic point of view, are among the most incompetent we have ever had. Trudeau is doubtless very good in certain areas, but he and his entourage are almost completely opposite to what are usually termed good economic managers.

In trying to come to grips with Quebec's structural weaknesses, we cannot, within the present context, act in place of the federal government. We can only, in addition to the role of "firemen" which we currently play as a result of a number of urgent matters, develop immediate, short-term programs, trying to make them a little less seasonal, and in some instances where we control the determinant levers, try to build programs which will create permanent jobs. We are working incessantly in this area—in asbestos, in steel, in agrobusiness (where we have an extremely low level of self-sufficiency in relation to our potential). The climate is not an insurmountable problem precluding, for example, cattle rearing from developing in Quebec. The proportion of beef cattle and sheep we import would be largely reduced if we could produce for ourselves enough to meet our own needs. It is just as cold in the Canadian west and the American west as it is in Quebec!

I think that Quebec can do something to change its position within the straightjacket imposed by market forces which are out of our control. But to image that we could change it as we would like is a utopian fantasy as long as the current regime persists.

Do the Quebec unions appear to you to be less tough as a result of the persisting economic crisis and increasing unemployment?

No, but there is one thing that should not be forgotten: we have the unprecedented advantage of not owing anything to the unions. We must keep this advantage. Our hands are not in any way tied as far as the unions are concerned. We asked them for nothing during the ten years it took to build this party, taking the seedling, strengthening its roots and bringing it to power. We owe not a cent, not a dollar, to the employers, or to the unions, nor to any of these pressure groups which are legitimate, but too often prone to exaggerate when they get a chance. We have no organic ties, which means that we can be the government of all the people without being a puppet to any one sector. I should bring in at this point the very intimate ties we have with what is known as the "grassroots." I often have the impression that we are closer to this base of workers than those who officially speak on their behalf. This was very clearly shown in the results of the 1976 elections. And our government must maintain a prejudice in favor of the workers.

Are you not underestimating the leftism of the unions?

The trade unions are occasionally politicized, which is not in the North American tradition. They are sometimes even "marxized." But a deeper current, which makes much less noise, ensures a certain stability. The refusal to overstate one's case is very strong among individuals in Quebec, and it lies deeper than one imagines. I am not saying that we should accept this value and refuse to make changes. But if we lean gently against this quality in our society, the changes will come peacefully. From the beginning we have tried to establish conditions for a new departure within the current social climate. "New contract" would certainly be a presumptuous phrase! But more than ever before we have need of clarity and of good faith in the field of labor relations. The state, through legislation which innovated fairly vigorously without turning everything upside down, and especially through its behavior, has attempted to set a tone. The results have been encouraging: 1977 was quieter than 1976. But the hardest tests are still to come.

If we can maintain our equilibrium and our contact with the stable and thoughtful currents in our society, we can cross this hurdle.

What were the results of the Malbaie summit which you organized a few months after you came into power?

We took the risk that our initial results would not be spectacular. We knew that even before we started. We organized the meeting of top economic decision makers called the "Malbaie summit." And since then, in a more precise, more sectoral, and at the same time more professional, way others have been organized. This does not achieve miracles from one day to the next. But it can trigger off some correction to rather frantic appetites and thinking on the sides both of prices and profits, and of incomes. We must make it clear that we are responsible for our collective economic health. This profitability is the only way in which we can improve the viability of our society as a whole. We must have a growing cake if we are to be able to better divide it. There will always be differences and confrontations in any democratic society where interest groups retain the right to organize and negotiate. But without an essential minimum of solidarity on certain obvious points of common interest, without which everyone is the loser, there is no progress possible. We are searching for these basic common interests and we will continue to search patiently, because these ditches are old and deep and the habit of dialogue somewhat lost.

One of the first laws voted by your government concerned the visibility of party financing. It could be thought that you are pursuing a moralistic cause more urgently than the political and economic emancipation expected by your electorate.

Without wishing to make Quebec the only pure corner of the world, because we know well enough that we are no angels, let me bring up the subject of the kickback affairs in the United States, in Japan, and in Italy and those a little better hidden but suspected in certain large Canadian public companies abroad. Political morality matters too. The multinationals must follow the laws and regulations of the countries in which they operate. They must be forced to desist if, on occasion, they exercise undue influence, and help to feed the over-extensive corruption in the western political and administrative world.

Certainly we have our weaknesses too, but we have, nonetheless, during ten years of political activity before arriving in government, given ourselves a strict tradition which is without equal, and probably without precedent in the contemporary western world. One of the first laws we signed, Law No. 2, goes a long way, not only on the subject of the obligatory divulgence of their sources of revenues by the parties, but also in excluding any subscription from companies, businesses and trade unions. We want the elector, the taxpayer, to have an individual responsibility and an integral right to either make or to unmake governments.

Refusing to sell oneself at the state level is one of the fundamental conditions of political emancipation and economic dignity.

In which sectors does Quebec want to affirm its presence?

First, in all the cultural industries—which will be of ever-increasing importance—such as communications, the large news media, publishing, etc. This is not a question of "marshalling" information or thought, but we want the ownership of this sector to be well and truly rooted in Quebec, with very clear rules of play.

Another more topical example: the primary steel industry. The V.S. Canadian steel complex situated around the Great Lakes has obtained excessive influence through maintaining "Great Lakes prices" for the sale of steel. In order to break this cartel and give our utilizing industries a chance not to pay excessive transportation costs, we are insisting that our principal steel industry should remain the collective property of Quebec, until the day when it is sufficiently solid and we can make it a mixed enterprise.

We also foresee leaving a free market for the majority of consumer goods, but on condition that foreign business allow sufficient Quebec participation for their books to remain open to us, and for a member of the board to fulfill the function of "public director." This will not be an honorary title. This director will be fully trained to defend the public interest and prevent foreign businesses behaving like foreign bodies in our society. This is a very, very brief summary, a glimpse of what we have chosen to do in preparation for the day when Quebec, unlike the rest of Canada which has been neglectful, will be able to assert its desire for both political and economic emancipation without either disruption or extravagant spending.

Since your arrival in office have you felt any reservations on the part of financial circles?

Yes, there were some at first. Many observers, with a hidden smile, followed my first sortie as leader of the Quebec government, which was as you know in New York at the Economic Club. I wanted to describe very frankly and very clearly what we wanted to do, what were the essential elements in our program. I confirmed our objective of "sovereignty-association" with Canada, and then I specified the main outlines of our economic and social program. The reason I accepted in January 1977 to go to New York was that I wished to dispel the sense of wavering, the incertitude which financial circles always feel when there is any change of government. These people wanted to become acquainted with us. The classical way to achieve this was to go and meet them. However, added to this normal feeling, in the case of the Parti Québécois, was a heavy air of malaise, partly instinctive and partly fed by propaganda generated by our Anglo-Canadian friends. In fact the victory of the P.Q. was presented as an announcement of secession. All the innuendos surrounding this word automatically created a movement of recoil in the United States, because it invoked old images of their Civil War. In order to dispel some of the confusion, I therefore went to New York. My speech had negative after effects in some places, especially in Toronto and in English Canada where they acknowledge none of our objectives, but I think that what I said helped to clarify things in the United States.

Will the size of Quebec's natural resources prevent any limit to its growth rate?

We do not foresee that Quebec, under existing world conditions, could have a growth rate any greater than other countries.

Let us look at our position: one of the problems of growth is linked to energy. We are among one of the world's greatest consumers of imported petroleum. And in as far as we can calculate Quebec's share in the Canadian account, our balance of payments is catastrophic. The energy consumption of our population of six million in Quebec will double between now and the 1980s, which will bring our annual petroleum bill alone to several billions of dollars!

Our enormous consumption is a result of the fact that we are among the most extravagant consumers of energy—because of the enormity of our distances, and the communication requirements imposed on six million people spread over this immense territory. This naturally means that our automobiles travel long distances. Our climate is extreme also; our weather conditions which, granted, are experienced by all northern countries, mean a high consumption of fuel. We are therefore thinking very seriously about economizing on energy, for example by improving the insulation of houses, which have always been built as though our sources of energy were inexhaustible and our means of payment unlimited. The fact is that the specific needs of our economy "burn" 75 per cent of our energy, which is derived entirely from imported petroleum. Currently our petroleum comes almost exclusively from Venezuela, with a few shipments from the Middle East and some small supplies from western Canada. But we think that this delicate, and barely adequate, source of supply may be upset within a few years. The pipeline will not run from the west to the east, but from the importing east to the west, which will soon lack resources. Certainly there are the bituminous sands in Alberta, but the cost of exploring them is so exorbitant that we cannot count on them. How can we give a specific answer to our growth problems given these facts?

There is a whole gamut of means open to us, one of which is the better utilization of energy, and this implies working on people's minds. It would be necessary, for example, to reserve the roads in the rush hours to cars carrying at least three or four people. This implies a gradual, and perforce partial, policy of replacing petroleum, which to a large extent could be done by electricity. We have enormous hydroelectric resources, but they will provide only for the growth in consumption envisaged between now and the late '80s at the latest.

However, this does allow us to take a step back from nuclear power, which presents many dangers. We are still far from knowing all the uncertainties, all the consequences, all that in the future may make us regret too hasty a decision. We prefer to move slowly in that area. We have only two nuclear power stations: one is experimental and a second under construction—plus a third which is still at the planning stage. Having passed through the initial stages which allowed us to develop our skills and keep ourselves abreast of the scientific and technical changes affecting this sector, we have no wish to plunge headlong into nuclear power. Our present situation will allow us to sit back for a few years during which time we will observe—because research is continuing both in the rest of the world and here—and perhaps we will find less disquieting forms of energy.

Is Quebec a producer of uranium?

No. Bourassa was a little ahead of himself a few years ago, in Paris, when he spoke like a minor, newly rich uranium tycoon. As far as energy resources, which are indispensable and which are at the center of the combustion process are concerned, we have plenty; but uranium we have to bring from elsewhere. However, more intensive and better planned research has recently given more serious, rather than merely hopeful, indications of possible beds in our northern regions.

Like everyone, we are searching. We must certainly also work on solar and wind power. We must also look for petroleum, but our ancient ground, the "Shield," is not a very good source of hydrocarbons. In any case we will have to have, as other countries do, an energy policy which will put certain limits on what we traditionally call growth.

Does energy policy derive from the provincial or the federal government?

It is a vast jungle. There are federal regulations concerning exportation. If we wish to sell seasonal surpluses of electricity to New York State, we have to obtain an export permit from the federal government.

As far as imports are concerned the story is practically the same, except that our imports are essentially petroleum goods, and they are most often dealt with by companies whose activities and policies seem to escape everyone to some extent.

Our party was the first to propose the creation of a "witness" sector, an idea which derives from certain European experiences. This public sector could be formed by purchasing or expropriating some of the companies which operate in our country, and organizing a state enterprise which would corner approximately 20 per cent of the market, from importation, to sale to the customers, including the refining process. That would at least allow us to keep an eye on the market and eventually to improve its regulation.

What policy do you plan to adopt for Quebec's primary resources: forestry, water, the mines?

As far as the forests are concerned, they constitute Quebec's greatest renewable resource, and we envisage retaining their exclusive ownership. However, we must distinguish between the resource—the forests—and the factories which have been established in Quebec by interests which draw their supplies of pulp and paper from here. It would be foolish to break up this vertical integration. Why should we buy up mills which are already, in many cases, rather out of date and which need to be modernized, in order to sell the same paper to the same "interests"? Our forest resources are our promise of a good future. Apart from the classic utilization of wood there are many new areas of development. This demands that we retrieve the administration and management of the resource, in order to break the system of concessions in perpetuity, or almost perpetuity, which was traditionally practiced in Quebec.

As far as the mines are concerned there are more nuances to the situation. There are three mining sectors in Quebec. I was the minister responsible for the mines for long enough to know that asbestos is a very special case. We are the largest exporters of asbestos in the world. But there are also converting and utilization sectors. Asbestos being a resource not widely found in the world, we could easily take over total or partial control without risking much confusion. The same does not apply, for example, to the nonferrous sector, such as silver, gold or copper in which today it is very difficult to maintain production. The price of copper is nearly always floating as a result of speculative maneuvering on a very fragile international market.

The case of iron ore is different again. As a result of the concentration techniques developed in the 1950s, iron ore has become the most common mineral in the world. What was called rock before these recent discoveries can now, by means of a wholly mechanical system of concentration which does not even call for any complicated procedures, become 70 per cent iron. Neither Quebec nor any other country has exclusive rights to this system. We must therefore take care not to lose our existing markets and remain in very close contact with our American neighbors who are our principal market.

We have an abundance of known resources, and new methods of aerial detection have enabled us to identify further beds to be exploited, which confirm that iron ore is an almost inexhaustible resource for Quebec.

Quebecers have been called the asbestos Arabs ...

Asbestos does not have the prestige of petroleum. It is a primary substance which is mostly discussed, justifiably, because of asbestosis. It nonetheless remains one of the substances the economy currently could not do without. It enters, to a greater or lesser degree, into the composition of hundreds of products.

The step that we have decided to take is to assume control of one of the large companies in order that the state can become more or less a co-proprietor of the sector. This will give us the leverage which will allow us to "maximize" conversion and therefore the creation of jobs in Quebec. Otherwise it would all remain in the hands of a few foreign multinationals. Not that these companies always have that monstrous side that is so often attributed to them. On the other hand, we should not underemphasize their influence nor the dangers they represent, especially if we are weak in our dealings with them. I do not understand, or dare not understand, why so many governments give the impression of literally trembling before the multinationals. In the case of asbestos we had to act, and we did so without hesitation. The sources of our electoral funds are no secret. We have not compromised ourselves with any multinational.

What sectors in particular will you concentrate on?

The manufacturing sector gives us the most concern. We have "soft" sectors which demand substantial rationalization and conversion, which is always a painful operation. The pulp industry will remain powerful providing the mills are modernized rapidly. Many of the mills have been allowed to age, as a result, perhaps, of an overdose of self-satisfaction, because we were, along with the Scandinavian countries, the largest suppliers of pulp in the world. But other countries have grown. The United States discovered that it had the capacity. It had a cheap labor market still available among the black population in the South, a climate favoring the growth of trees, and a lesser requirement for quality—these young trees do not give the same sort of paper as trees that have had sixty years to mature—but they are replaced more quickly.

Therefore while others were active, here we remained self-satisfied with an industry we were allowing to become outdated.

Could you assess your position now, or sketch a rapid balance sheet, after two years in power?

Let us go, very briefly, back to November 15, 1976. I was in my constituency which is one of the most highly populated in Quebec, and which is part of the metropolitan south bank of the Saint Lawrence near Montreal. I had just returned from a five week tour which had taken me throughout almost all Quebec. Like many people I had the impression that the situation was developing as it had never done before. Some of our polls even went as far as to predict victory. I must say that I did not believe them. During the whole election day, on November 15, like all candidates do, I walked from one polling station to another to encourage the volunteers who were working there, either counting or supervising. During the course of the day I had prepared three small pieces of paper. On the first I had written "Defeat." Defeat, for us, signified having very positive results from the francophone electorate, but failing as a result of an electoral system which did not favor us. This could still give us 5 or 10 seats out of the 110 in the Assembly.

I looked at this piece of paper and I put it on one side. I told myself that this time we should be victorious. So I took the second piece of paper, which I labelled: "Victory," and which I had prepared for the prospect of 30 or 40 seats in the Assembly, which seemed to me to be the maximum threshold we could cross. However, I was afraid, as many of us were in the party, that once again, as in 1970 and 1973, there would be a sort of recoil at the last minute, and that our opponents' propaganda would be successful in its purpose, announcing the end of the world, the apocalypse and terror in the event of a victory by the P.Q. The third piece of paper I labelled:

"Miracle." This supposed that we won power. I confess that I had written absolutely nothing on this piece of paper. I didn't believe it possible. Towards eight o'clock when the results began to come in, some friends came over to find me: "You can bring out your 'Miracle' paper, because it's happening." I confess I was stupified. Ten years is, after all, a very short time in which to give birth to, enlarge and establish a political party, the Parti Québécois, and also dislodge a machine as ancient, rich and deeply entrenched as the Liberal one.

We were all immensely happy. But I also felt a certain amount of fear which was not completely unjustified. We had won overwhelming responsibility which had arrived suddenly and almost prematurely. After ten years one has the impression of having waited a very long time, but when a party arrives in power and becomes an instrument of government, ten years seems a very short time in which to become completely prepared. I asked myself whether we were ready to assume this burden. But one thing I am certain of: I am sure that the leader of a party, obliged to appoint ministers, has never experienced an equal degree of embarrassment by being faced with such a wealth of human resources.

We have now been working for two years, a period which I will divide into three—overlapping, obviously—stages. First, putting the house in order. For instance, less than one month after our accession to power, we needed an emergency session before Christmas, because we had to stop some holes. There were holes amounting to some $200,000,000, in the city of Montreal's Olympic debts alone. This was a very big problem. Some problems had been left unsolved during the campaign, as is always the case. For example, it was necessary, before December 31, to renew the law on the administration of rented properties, which normally expired each year. In addition we had to begin to prepare a supplementary budget immediately to carry us through the end of the government's budgetary year, to March 31.

Putting the house in order also meant preparing the spring 1977 budget, reorganizing the loan situation and, as far as possible, alleviating the unemployment crisis. In other words we had to pilfer as much as we could from the budget, our first economic operation, in order to find some tens of millions with which to try and plug some of the most painful holes in the unemployment area. We wanted at least to try, with all the means available to a province (because we do not have substantial means) and we had to use those means to the maximum. We basically, therefore, had to reduce our rate of borrowing and bring down an austere budget. There was no other way out after what happened at the time of the Olympics. We managed to find $80,000,000 immediately in the spring for short-term employment . . . or at least to try and reduce the problem, while maintaining Quebec's credit-worthiness which could have been endangered had we not tightened our belts and given an example of moderation to the international lending market. Remember that during the previous two or three years Canada, with its twenty-three million inhabitants, had become the largest borrower in the western world, and Quebec had been the greatest contributor to this frightening rise in borrowing. We had to reduce this increasing rate of borrowing. This is what we aimed for in what I call our first period, or our organization period, or rather, our emergency reorganization period.

The second stage began with the 1977–78 session and the budget that followed. This did not mean that we forgot about the reorganization, and that we did not continue to watch it closely. But in the second stage we were able to make our "social-democratic" mark in different sectors, as a government, on the administration and on legislation. We began to do things more specifically related to what we had promised, and to try to be a good government, or as we have been hired to be, a real provincial government, until the order of things changed. What I find the most significant in this stage and which, I believe, is related to a particular way of seeing the progress of society, was the need to fulfill a pledge which had prevailed in Quebec, from party to party, and from government to government for many years: we had to regulate, once and for all, the financing of political parties. On the political level this is fundamental, for the democratic system requires that individual citizens should finance the parties, plus the state—providing it does so only to a modest extent—from the public purse. It is essential that the sources of party funds be made public, be brought out of the wings. On this front I think that we have in some way been pioneers among the western countries, and I am rather proud of it. I always rate this achievement high; and I hope that it has come to stay. I am thinking, for example, of the Liberals . . . I am still waiting to receive the breakdown of the contributions in Mr. Ryan's leadership fund. But to all intents and purposes the party has agreed freely, it seems, to play the game according to Law No. 2. From now on the law applies to them just as to everyone else and the Liberal party must, from now on, evaluate its funds and make public the sums which arrive in its account—and the sources of these funds. Otherwise we will never be able to operate in any sort of democratic manner.

I also want to mention the whole social side. When one is sure that a change is basically right—in other words, that one is going in the right direction—one can always be tractable enough about details of implementation. Automobile insurance is a good example of the social policy we have attempted to realize. We voted in the law last year, just before Christmas Eve, and it came into force in the spring. One has to allow oneself a certain amount of time; first one must have the law in order to have the right to acquire the necessary budget to put the law into operation. We gave ourselves until March 1 to bring the law into force so that motorists could take advantage of it during 1978. After Christmas when I went on a tour, as soon as question time began in the meetings invariably a dozen people came to the microphone. At least eight of them would be there to tell me how their agents had told them it was the end of the world, that it would not work, that they were worried, that it would be chaotic. We asked ourselves where we were going; the reaction was alarming. March 1 arrived. A few months afterwards, by the beginning of the autumn, the more it continued, the more we were proved right. I could go to all sorts of meetings in which there were many other questions, and many other problems, but no one was talking about automobile insurance any more.

Now, in fact, people can make comparisons. There are people who were insured under the old system who are still in the courts. They have waited for five or six years and have never seen a dime. While now, at the end of one or two months at the maximum—providing the accident reports are clear—those who have a right to benefits begin to receive them. They could, in some cases, receive them until the end of their days. I think that any major change—there are, after all, more than three million people driving on our roads—which contains complex aspects, which requires the application of a method, is frightening . . . until the day one sees the results. Motor insurance is a good example. Sovereignty-association is also a method on many levels. It consists of fundamental questions which affect the normal pride of a society, but there are also many practical, economic, etc., problems involved. It is normal for people to be anxious, as they were over the question of automobile insurance; but I am sure (as are those working with us) that basically we are not making a mistake. This is the direction in which Canada and Quebec must move. Six months or a year after it is decided, we will wonder how we managed to be so wound up about it.

On the cultural side there has been Law 101. I think that with this law we have succeeded at least in clarifying and working into a more vigorous format what was initiated under pressure by the Bourassa government's Law 22. And I think that now there is a good chance that it will be permanent. In this second stage we have tried to make our mark in different sectors. Take, for example, Law 45 which amends the Labor Code and deals with the notorious strike-breakers' problem. Or the consumer who, between now and the end of 1978, will benefit from new legislation. In all these areas we are trying to realize what our program and our promises implied: action by a government with a vision of the future, and a government which will maintain its resolve. The 1978–79 budget moved in the same direction. The key to this budget was its social content. Average income earners have been milked by successive governments, one after the other, because they are "them," the mass. We have been able to ensure this group a substantial lowering of taxation. On the other hand, at the other extreme, among high income earners we have had to raise the level and there has been an increase in taxation. I think that this was normal. We had to relieve, as quickly as possible, the working mass of the population, which makes ends meet with difficulty, which is struggling against inflation, and against taxation; we had to give these people some respite, and I think that what we have done has been fairly substantial. If you add to that what we have done for old people. . . . Free medication is important to them. Often at the end of the month they have to make the incredible choice between their grocery basket or medication.

Another major aspect of our second stage was its economic content. We live in a world in which economics has always been important, and in which it is going to become more and more complicated. Whether we want it or not, for as long as we live, economic problems, the economic situation, will be permanent emergencies which will be increasingly difficult to resolve. Quebec has an open economy. We import a lot, we export a lot; the two must be kept in balance as well as possible. Principally because of our petroleum imports, we have a balance of payments deficit. This will have to be corrected. Everything to do with the economy is a central preoccupation, and it is necessarily so. The economic cake must be large enough to allow us to realize all the social and cultural policies we wish to introduce. From this point of view we have had to face the problem of trying to combine urgency with, if you like, a certain minimum medium-term perspective. Two things were urgent: several tens of millions of dollars as fast as possible to try to stimulate employment, and now what we call OSE* (operation economic solidarity) which had demanded much more preparation, and which will last until spring of 1979 or perhaps even longer. This has helped in a number of sectors which we have already identified; it has created or maintained, I think, around thirteen or fourteen thousand jobs. At the same time we had to work on the medium term, for example on asbestos policy. It had been discussed for ten years; it was time for a policy to materialize. The same applies to the pulp and paper industry where for a long time many mills had been allowed to become run down, and there were some closures. We had to try and draw up, between the companies, between the employees, and the government, a proposal for revival and for growth. The same applies also in the so-called soft sectors, i.e., the traditional sectors such as textiles, clothing, shoes and furniture; and our discussions culminated in the decision we made on the sales tax when that unilateral initiative arrived from Ottawa. They wanted to cut 3 per cent across the board. We said no: if there were going to be cuts we would make them ourselves. Our first considera- tion was the social needs of families: furniture, shoes, clothing, which are needed almost everyday, throughout the year. You know the quibbling that followed. But I think that seeing the tax fall from 8 per cent to zero for a year, rather than to 5 per cent for six months, gave vital fresh air to a whole sector of our economy, and I think that this measure helped the people too.

In addition I will simply underline, within the whole economic sphere, the importance of agriculture, or rather agrobusiness, agriculture which is production, business which is conversion, distribution, market-place, consump- tion. This is a vital sector because, whether we like it or not, it will take on more and more importance between now and the year 2000. A society which does not feed its people properly is

*Opération de solidarité économique

a disgrace. We have made agrobusiness a primary concern; very soon we will have to do something that will be very difficult. This goes back to something I said about auto insurance. We are sure now, that the base, the foundations, are good—this is an appropriate term because we are dealing with the land, with the protection of agricultural land, with zoning. This will happen before the end of 1978. There will probably be cries from certain corners, particularly from those who will see the writing on the wall for their speculative ventures or happy-go-lucky construction projects. Construction must take place elsewhere than on our best land. This is a question not only of helping the farmers today, but of protecting our arable inheritance, because the more time passes, the more we will need it.

Finally the third stage, which has begun. This does not mean that the first two are not continuing, but that the third also has finally started. We had put a sort of relative moratorium on all activity relating to the referendum and sovereignty-association—with the exception of passing the referendum law. We have not undertaken, shall we say, much new evangelism; but we have not forgotten the objective. For almost a year and a half it was necessary for us to put this subject in the background, because it would not have seemed very responsible on our part to have travelled around the country like busybodies preaching the essential future— but the future nonetheless—while appearing to neglect the present, and the immediate problems to be resolved. Since this last summer, and particularly at the beginning of autumn 1978, we have been able I think to collect our ideas once again on the subject. We have started what we are calling our "pre-referendum organization," that is, the mobilization of our membership which we are going to try to increase as systematically as possible. Because we have a damnable problem vis-à-vis the referendum. We have promised—and we must keep to this promise—that the referendum will take place outside the electoral period, before the next general election, which means that when the referendum approaches its official campaign period, we will be obliged to fulfill the roles of both government and preachers of our idea. It is for this reason that we will have to count to such an extent on militants from the party. We, on our side, will do our part. We will risk reorganizing our days and encroaching to the maximum on our leisure time. In general, when one leaves for a major general campaign such as for elections, one leaves the deputy-minister in charge and goes out into the country. The government disappears for a month or six weeks except for one or two Cabinet meetings or for emergencies, and it wages an electoral campaign. For weeks, for maybe two or three months, as long as this officially lasts, we will have to do our work, and campaign with the others. This is a problem which has not been resolved.

PART 3

Sovereignty-Association

After two years in power, and ten years of sovereignty-association, has there been any evolution in your political and social philosophy?

Without going into any analysis of our internal evolution and what has happened on the surface, I would say that it is as if we have fastened the buckle. Eleven years ago, when I arrived at the Liberal party congress with the idea of sovereignty-association, they refused even to discuss the subject. Therefore, in 1967, some of us left. This led to what is known as the Sovereignty-Association Movement, and eleven years ago this year, in 1968, this new group was eventually christened the Parti Québécois. For myself, I have always believed in our option, and I think that our only future is in that direction. For example, I was reading the latest book by one of the greatest European economists, Francois Perroux, who has reached the age of about seventy, an age when one begins to do one's summing up. His book deals with two notions which are becoming more and more inevitable in the world, namely the independence of the nation and the interdependence of nations. Evolution occurs in a curious way.

You know that shortly after the creation of our party, the RIN with Bourgault, Allemagne, and others was officially disbanded. Their members were advised to join the Parti Québécois in order to avoid dividing their forces. Many of them arrived like pioneers who had, completely, selflessly, already devoted several years of their lives to the idea, to the cause, if you like. They arrived with sometimes a less-than-total degree of acceptance of what we were proposing. In effect, they have always had a sort of "pure and fast" idea of independence deep in themselves—and I can understand how this happens in those who are obliged to be pioneers, to break open barred windows, to cry out loud in the streets because no one listened at the beginning. And this spirit was evident at many of our congresses in the form of efforts to find means of bringing as close together as possible the ideas of sovereignty or independence on the one hand, and diluting or eliminating or reducing the idea of association on the other. There was therefore some wavering from the top to the bottom of the organization. In 1975, for example, there was a congress at which the majority of the pressure was exercised around the idea of the referendum. For those who had, by that time, been thinking of independence, working for independence, for twenty years of their lives, it was hard to accept the idea of a step such as this. However, it finally went through and I think it was a step we had to go through. Today, after several months of consultation, we reached agreement among ourselves at Cabinet level, at Parliamentary caucus level, and at the level of the executive council of the party, and I think that the time was opportune to come forward with the statement I made to the National Assembly. To us, this declaration marked the point we had reached. This means that, in essence, we have returned to the position we first took. And I think that there is no other viable perspective of our future possible: clearly defined association in two or three essential areas, and sovereignty everywhere else. What we will retain in common with Canada is a continuity, which will be largely economic, but also political. This continuity will be political at least in the following sense: if we were to break off all relations with Canada, we would become a body that would be not only different, but hostile, between Ontario and the maritimes—we would turn ourselves into a ghetto with the animosity we would create around us. We must therefore maintain an area of common ground and continuity between us. The interdependence of the world tells us that it makes good sense for all neighboring countries to preserve things in common with each other in this way. We have identified three basic factors here: the market, which we had agreed to ten years ago; currency, which we anticipated ten years ago; and finally—and this belongs more in the continental context—taking our natural place in the alliances such as NATO and NORAD, that is to say in continental and Atlantic security, the security of the world of which we are a part. I think that all this is now accepted in principle. At least, this is what came out of our meetings this summer and at the beginning of the autumn.

What is still causing some disturbance is the fact that I took it upon myself—and it was necessary to do so—to specify that we would have to have a referendum which would cover the two areas: sovereignty and association. By definition, this implies negotiation. In a situation where one is talking of keeping some things in common and separating the rest, obviously civilized people will negotiate. The mandate we will be given at the referendum will therefore be to negotiate. Some people consider that this is too weak, but as far as I am concerned, and I think I will probably exhaust myself by repeating it, it is not too weak. It will be magnificent if Quebec replies: "yes, we want this!" It will be magnificent because it will mean that there is a desire for sovereignty, as defined, plus association, as defined. I have the impression that we will not need two referendums. The rest of Canada will hear us, whatever the government in Ottawa. There are those who feel a certain degree of reticence at the idea of association. . . . They have not followed the evolution of today's world closely . . . nor the evolution of the political context. They have retained too absolute an idea. That is their right, but we are not obliged to follow them into that particular fray. The rest of our reservations are perhaps the result of nothing more than a complex we may have because we have never passed by this way before; we still think of ourselves as colonials, which makes us question the importance of a massive "yes" in Quebec. In Europe, in the United States, everywhere, they won't go inspecting the plumbing. When they talk about Quebec they will say: "Look, the

Quebecers said yes. What did they say yes to? To sovereignty and association." This is what a "yes" means. And it carries extraordinary weight. I think that going back to the source of the movement, and succeeding in defining the essentials, has placed us in as good a position as we would humanly be in, in relation to the referendum and its sequel. I cannot prophesy the sequel but, deep down, I am sure that we are going in the right direction. This certainty is shared by all those who have been consulted over the past few weeks and months. On our side anyhow, basically everything is clear.

You must have read the criticism made on the subject. Marcel Adam, for example, thought your strategy very skilful, but Bourgault thought it a step backward. Where will the members of the party stand?

Certainly there has been some backlash. You make a declaration that is fairly complex, and then you are called on to explain its effects, as happened on this occasion at a press conference. In the newspapers the following day the head-lines corresponded more or less to what was said, especially that the conference had lasted for an hour and a half. This is natural—it is like when a slightly complicated new law is tabled. For a long period of time there have been people saying: "Wait a minute. What is this leading to?" But they have not read the text, they read only the headlines and then they hear someone, whether it be M. Bourgault or anyone else, protest certain aspects of the law. It is normal; they are worried. Those who follow things more closely, who take the trouble to dig deeper, see things differently . . . for example, those, who possess remarkable social and national conscience like Pierre Vadeboncoeur. He waited several days before writing an article in *Le Devoir* which is concise, well thought-out and which says: if there is another strategy possible which would not automatically lead to conflict, let it be known. It takes time to decant an idea. M. Bourgault, I believe, is one of those I mentioned just previously. Many among these people are still tied to the idea of absolute sovereignty; and as for association, they tend to ask what it is when it is at home. I am therefore convinced that they have not taken the trouble to study its implications, at least, not yet. This would explain why, every time they are told that it may perhaps take several years, they have the impression that it is a step backwards. My own view is that if we do not proceed in this way, it will not be a question of it taking several years, but we will risk, purely and simply, coming to grief by proposing something that is completely unrealizable. At that moment they will look for another movement for themselves, and either through stupidity, or through miscalculation, we will have created a sense of demoralization which could last for years and years, perhaps a generation. We do not have the right to fail deliberately. Let them cry— electoralism! It would be very natural for any member of Parliament, any minister, especially one who is young, to think in this way, to feel that he still has a lot of time in which to do his best work. However, one thing is certain: it has never entered into our discussions that delaying the referendum could make the next elections easier for us. We are not even thinking about the next election . . . at least officially. Some people may be thinking about it secretly, but I am not. I have been in this trade for eighteen years now; and I have no federal ambition. I could never go any further in politics. I feel that my job, essentially—and I know there are others within our group who think the same way—is to do the maximum possible to achieve the results required. I would like to see this in my lifetime. And in order to get the results one has to avoid stupid mistakes: it is as simple as that.

What kind of route will you suggest to the party?

We do not have to propose a special route to the party. The party, after all, is used to being a democratic party, and it is very jealous of its internal prerogatives which will allow it to study the matter in December. At the beginning of December there will be what we call a national council, which happens three or four times a year. After the December meeting people in each region will meet to prepare for the congress which will take place in May next year. This system is prescribed in the party regulations and it will give people the opportunity to examine and evaluate everything in minute detail. They will make their decision, subsequently, at the Congress, where they will decide what attitude they should take. For myself, I have enormous confidence in the maturity of the party. The immense majority of our members are serious people, and for this reason I think that during the next few months we will see increasing clarity in our position.

Is the congress a way of up-dating your program?

Yes, every time. Now it happens every two years. Previously it was every year, perhaps because we needed to follow the progress of our business more closely. But since 1975 it has been every two years. Our 1979 congress will be decisive because it will be the last congress before the referendum.

When you describe the new political formula which will allow Quebec to feel more free, you avoid using the word "independence" even more than the term "separatism." You readily talk of "sovereignty-association." This leads one to believe that you are returning to the slogan of the movement you created under this name, in 1967. Is this a step back on your part, or a tactical maneuver?

Not at all. Neither. I use these words more frequently because, since 1968, they have been the master keys to our action: sovereignty and association. I break away from them on occasion only in order to illustrate a point through drawing analogies, but without varying the basic assumptions. The word "separatism," which alludes to a brutal rupture, is much too negative a term for what we are proposing. From the beginning of our fight we have continually reiterated that geography and a whole series of obvious interests prescribe that association with Canada must be parallel with the independence of Quebec. It would be a crime to cripple, with one blow, two centuries of communal co-existence. Even if we wanted to, we could probably not do it. Canada is a "Common Market" as advantageous, if not more so, for Ontario as for Quebec.

Today, do you carry the sovereignty or independence label?

Sovereignty, independence? Let us be clear that the difference is only in nuance. "Independence" is more political. The term certainly covers the central part of our option, political sovereignty. In practice the two concepts meet. Having used the two words, my preference today is clearly for "sovereignty." Each to his taste. But the idea of an association has to be added to that of "self-government."

This would therefore be an economic type of association?

Many other angles are possible over and above the economic association, based on a customs union, which will be the beginning: a maritime community to manage navigation up the Saint Lawrence to the Great Lakes; interdependence in the monetary domain—which would avoid many of the problems of the EEC. Many common areas are possible, some narrower than others, some wider. We could go as far as the abolition of exclusive citizenship, to the creation of joint passports. Defense arrangements can be made, including our joining NATO. Obtaining a seat in the United Nations goes without saying. We are fighting for the freedom to defend a national dimension for ourselves. However, Quebec has no reason to cease membership in the Commonwealth if it succeeds in extracting itself from the traditional politics of Ottawa, and some of Canada's traditional ties.

Another example: instead of throwing Quebec into the development of ruinously expensive international airlines, why not follow the example of the Scandinavians and practice a common policy in this area of communications? This can all be part of a future package which can be developed conjointly, providing the point of departure is good. Without bickering. At the proper time.

M. Trudeau once said: "It is an illusion, Quebec wants nothing. It is not lacking in power but in savoir-faire." Do you not think that your economic plans could be compatible with the current federal structure?

Oh! I could quote you Talleyrand who, at the time of the French revolution, had been living for two years in America. He said that remaining master in one's own home was the most important thing for a country. Anything Trudeau and all the others say can change nothing. The exercise of self-determination is absolutely necessary to the maturity of a society which possesses its own identity. However, interdependence does exist. I do not mean that a country should assume its responsibilities as if it were in a ghetto, cutting itself off from others. But if a society which is conscious of its identity, and which really feels itself to be a cohesive group, and therefore different from the others, does not go through at least a certain part of its history with the attributes of sovereignty, it will always remain a tainted society. It will be subject to a form of dependence in relation to the colonialism which formed it, and which is in fact preventing it from reaching maturity. Quebec must break this vicious circle.

The people of Quebec understand that the Canadian federal option would lead them, sooner or later, to submit to centralization. Even with a strong and effective Quebec administration, responsibility for the orientation of Quebec will revert to Ottawa, which by refining its methods of intervention will speak more and more in the name of "national" interest, and will control all major activities. The logic of the federal system calls for Ottawa to oppose Quebec's attempts at autonomy and continually cut off Quebec from any benefits won in a long history of conflict and occasional forcing of the issue.

The aims of the Parti Québécois have already been recorded in a series of attempts at reform made by every other government in Quebec, but none of them followed through to the logical end of their choice. This time I think we will be successful. Within the present federal framework, Quebec sovereignty is a contradiction in terms, a graft rejected by the Canadian political body. The independence we envisage will not be an autarchy; we will not cut ourselves off; we do not reject North American values. The independence we envisage is the only way possible to us because, as I said when I spoke to American businessmen in January 1977, "Canada and Quebec cannot continue to live like two scorpions in the same bottle," to borrow from Churchill's metaphor.

However, Quebec does possess some attributes of a nation-state. It has a flag and a National Assembly; it is recognized in some intergovernmental situations; it possesses almost diplomatic status, particularly with its general delegation in France; it legislates as it wishes in certain areas such as language and education. It therefore enjoys a margin of decision-making freedom and autonomy of action. Can we go back to the question debated in Ottawa since the end of the Second World War: "What does Quebec want?"

Would that the two founding peoples, the French Canadians and the English Canadians, could speak together on a one-to-one basis instead of in the majority-minority relationship which has always poisoned our political life. We are living with a system inspired by the American model, but imposed by Great Britain in the middle of the nineteenth century on the four colonies which then shared the Canadian territory: two maritime provinces, Ontario, and Quebec. Then, as the west opened up, five other provinces were added. Only

Newfoundland, after the Second World War, was consulted on its entry into the Federation.

But the system has remained warped: the number of provinces—whether it is four or ten—does nothing to alter the fact that two peoples founded Canada. Resistance by the francophone block, which has been evident since the nineteenth century, succeeded in slowing down evolution towards a unitarian centralized federalism. However, when the francophone population lost its numerical superiority and those in government in Ottawa wanted to govern Canada as a single nation, the federal system did, finally, become very centralized, and for almost half a century tension between the two blocks has been increasing. The federal system cooperates in maintaining Quebec in a state of economic underdevelopment and isolating it from decisions concerning its own future. This is a gift we can do without.

Every Quebec government since the beginning of the twentieth century has attempted intergovernmental guerilla warfare, but each time this has led to a federal counter-offensive which has given our history an appearance of having many ups and many downs. At the present time, given the level of Quebec's consciousness, it is not possible either in prudence or in moderation to follow the middle path according to such formulae as: "One state, two nations," "Cooperative or decentralized federalism," "Equality or Independence," "Cultural independence within economic federalism," etc. These are only electoral slogans, which mask the reality of a federal power which continues to function and to expand. It is time to choose between the Canadian option and the Quebec option.

Economic association between Canada and a sovereign Quebec has been categorically rejected by your colleagues, the provincial premiers. Are you therefore not tempted to look for an association with the United States?

First of all, no. And no! No to the annexation of Quebec by the United States! We are not going to leave a relatively limited power like Canada to fall into the arms of an all-devouring power like the United States. As far as I know the United States would have no interest in annexing our problems. I do not believe that the United States has imperialistic territorial ambitions as far as we are concerned. Nor do I see anywhere, except in the minds perhaps of some theorists, any ideas of annexation. This is obviously not to say that we would not be interested in developing more trade with our American neighbors, along with all that other north-south movement which is often the most logical. However, if economic association with Canada were to progress very slowly (which I think it will not), we would have to wait for this fit of bad humor to pass.

If we were to look simply at our internal trade, we would see that Ontario, by virtue of an industrial structure more developed, but also more dependent on capital than our own, is even more exposed to the risks of bad times. The greater the size of the investment, the greater the need for Quebec has tended to center its development, which it did not have much to say about, on consumer goods. Durable goods, such as household appliances and cars, come mostly from Ontario, where many large American groups have opened branch plants. Very close commercial ties exist between Ontario and Quebec. From a financial and economic point of view, Montreal is a suburb of Toronto, but in other respects it is Toronto that is the suburb of Montreal. They are two inter-related cities, reflecting a little the situation between Quebec and Ontario, with constant tension between the two but also with reciprocal links. If this common interest were negated, Ontario would suffer the most: for every two dollars worth of durable goods they sell to us, we sell them one dollar's worth. . . . But the goods sold by Quebec are those which one can less readily do without, which will render Quebec more able to withstand the blow should any longstanding debate hinder the conclusion of our agreements, while Ontario would very quickly feel its market crumbling if we were to withdraw our custom during the intervening period.

Just how far will you go to preserve Quebec's sovereignty, and avoid satellization by the United States?

The democratic tradition is very deeply rooted in the United States. The excesses of the war in Vietnam, Watergate, the CIA were extreme enough to make the United States take a necessary step back from their role as "the world's policeman." I hope I am not making predictions through rose-colored glasses by saying that it seems to me that the United States is abandoning over-rigid, and sometimes dangerous, policies. Today it seems to be moving towards a politics of concensus, especially with the countries it knows well. Consider the outcome of the Watergate affair. One has to ask oneself whether many countries in the world could have opened an internal wound with so great a degree of severity and harshness. The United States drew this courage from the heart of the very profound and sincere democratic tradition which has never left it.

Providing the will of the Quebec people is very clear, I see absolutely nothing (once the necessary adjustments have been made which will equip it with the institutions necessary for participation in continental life) that could preclude Quebec's survival and extremely fruitful survival. Take, for example, the Saint Lawrence Seaway: we plotted its course, we dug it out during the period of the "cold war" in order to prepare a protected entrance to the heart of the continent. It is per se a continental waterway: the mouth of the Saint Lawrence opens onto the sea, and one can travel on it as far as the Great Lakes. It was constructed across Quebec, since the Saint Lawrence runs through Quebec, and it is therefore, within the context in which we live, a joint property. The two proprietors of the massive complex of water constituted by the basin of the Great Lakes and its outlet, the Saint Lawrence, meet together to discuss it. If Quebec were to become independent, what reason would there be for Quebec not to become the third owner of this joint property? Who could prevent Quebec, with the two other partners, from managing this great expanse? Who could prevent Quebec, provided it pursued the democratic tradition, like Canada and the United States, from becoming a partner equally within the context of a democratic system which is, after all, the most solid in the world?

Suppose the United States chose Canada in preference to Quebec?

Like all the major powers, the United States is subject to temptation. They have given in to it very frequently. But following the enormous anguish of Vietnam, the revelations on Chile, and revelations on kick-backs in other countries, the United States is in the process of reawakening its conscience. President Carter has proved this with his appeals in support of the rights of man. Never mind that this is premature and a little presumptuous. What is important is that it reflects, over the last few years, a sort of internal purification of the American mentality, which seems to be trying progressively, laboriously, to return to its roots and become once again the flame of democracy. Will it really succeed?

One thing is for certain—the American attitude is much improved in relation to what it was twenty years ago. We could use this tendency as evidence to support our belief that the United States will respect our decision to become independent—which is not to say that they would immediately have a party on Wall Street! Especially if Quebec does not give concrete proof of its wish to be a solid partner in North American and Western dynamics. For example: since the 1976 elections I have on many occasions met Americans from the news media who were suddenly curious, which is not to say that they were not up-to-date on our affairs. In well-informed circles it was known that Quebec was developing but, when confronted with the event, many were surprised that it had happened so quickly. Among the most persistent questions, and also the most insidious, was one which constantly recurred: supposing Quebec were one day to become a sovereign state, what would be our attitude towards NORAD, that is, towards the North American air defense treaty. Even more insistent was the question of our attitude towards NATO. As often happens in a new party (ours has been in existence for only ten years) which wants to be progressive and which is trying to establish a certain break with the past, the P.Q. went quite far in isolationism. In 1969–70, during a congress, we voted, without any full explanation, withdrawal from NATO. This resolution was written into our program at one of those immature moments which every young party, which is also a party for change, goes through. But a political party, like a society, like a person to a certain extent, matures . . . and during the course of our congress in May 1977 we came to understand, simply because the threshold of power had been crossed, that we would have to adjust this position and remain open in our attitude towards NATO and NORAD. The same delegates who a few years ago were the ultra progressives voted very calmly to bring this subject back under question.

Do you foresee a need for national defense?

One of the permanent scandals of our civilization is that we cannot find the few billion necessary to relieve famine, but that we find hundreds of billions for the arms market. Fortunately Quebec is small. Fifteen per cent of the Canadian armed forces is made up of Quebecers, most of whom are located in bases situated in Quebec. If we rationalize these forces, and avoid all waste, we can supply Quebec's needs in the western alliance, which we have no intention of rejecting. It is also necessary to have troops to help to maintain a minimum of peace in the world. And also for internal security needs.

The Parti Québécois' program announced a presidential regime, a social system granting equal opportunity to all according to Quebec's means, and rapidly, but prudently, a degree of economic "repatriation." Is this an announcement of the nationalization of Quebec's economy?

Not at all. Economic repatriation will commence first of all with assembling all public revenues. An adult nation should control in particular its principal financial institutions. As far as chartered banks are concerned, current Canadian law provides more or less for this: foreigners and non-residents are not allowed to hold more than 25 per cent of the voting shares and identifiable shareholders do not have the right to hold more than 10 per cent. The law therefore establishes control over any foreign take-over in the banking system. The federal legislative structure and the accompanying regulations, clearly inspired by British tradition, have resulted in the Canadian banking system being dominated by five or six giants, none of which is of Quebec origin. Quebec has been able to maintain only two small banks, the *Banque canadienne nationale* and the *Banque provinciale,* which are dwarfs within the banking family. Fortunately, in addition to these two banks we have all the savings and credit unions, and the *Desjardins* movement, whose power is continually growing but which remains very minor in financial circles. What sovereignty would allow us to do would be to break this foreign constriction and forbid non-residents of Quebec and foreigners of any kind from owning more than 25 per cent of a bank. In a word, to repatriate control of our banking system.

Similarly, in insurance federal law provides that for every dollar received the company must invest at least $1,10 in order to guarantee its obligations. So far nothing out of the ordinary. However, this law applies to the whole Canadian territory. The money that is raised in Quebec is therefore not re-invested as it would be if one were to really take account of the dimension of the Province of Quebec. They have tried to persuade us that we are mistaken on this point, but we know that we are right. Quebec money, collected by the insurance companies, can easily go to Newfoundland, or to Labrador, or elsewhere in the west of Canada, into petroleum investments for example, and we have no real power to control such an accumulation of capital. And the only way we could achieve it is through sovereignty.

Foreign companies need not fear that we will present

them with an intransigent "nationalist" policy. When the time is right we will publish an investment code which will give a clear picture of those areas of our economy in which we will be willing to share control, and which foreign companies may remain in, or enter, on condition that they accept some Quebecers as managers.

In order to safeguard your independence vis-à-vis the business world, would it not be in your government's interest to practice a policy of financial autonomy? Are you not going to collide solidly against the narrowness of the Quebec financial markets?

The narrowness of the Quebec market corresponds with a population of only six million and, on the contrary, signifies that we do not have the problems of the 250 million Americans, or the 300 million Europeans, or even of the 25 million French. Quebec is a great producer of capital and of savings. It has enormous investment potential. In the present paracolonial context, in less than fifteen years, from 1961 to 1965, it exported nine billion dollars net which represents an enormous surplus for a society of six million people. But this haemorrhaging is, for the most part, the result of the fact that investments here are subject to too much foreign control. The Montreal stock market does not have the same vitality as that of New York, or even of Toronto. Our money all too often escapes the country. Sometimes it returns, under foreign control, to develop Quebec. This state of affairs, which is due to our lack of control over the gears in the investment machinery, and the circulation of savings and the accumulation of capital, must change. The Quebec tradition of saving is a strength, providing it is directed towards our own profit, and this should be possible with a new legislative and regulatory structure.

You often refer, as if to a model, to the Common Market. This is paradoxical. The European Economic Community, whose political content is limited, is going through a severe crisis. The nine countries feel that no major economic problems have been resolved.

When we consider the evolution of Europe since the signing of the Treaty of Rome, we cannot deny the progress and development the Common Market has permitted. Through opening up frontiers as never before, the Market has promoted a revolution absolutely without precedent in Europe. It has jolted some countries out of complacency and in consequence stimulated a certain amount of modernization and internal competition. It has contributed to the breaking up of traditional protectionist policies. It has stimulated the overall development of Europe. In addition it has helped to lessen much of the old, secular hate and animosity which prevailed across the continent. As a result of the opening of frontiers, a current of interrelations and reconciliation seems to have been established, which is much more natural, much more cordial, than ever before. This success seems to me to be extraordinarily sound and could be an important inspiration for Quebec and Canada.

Do you think, then, that Ottawa will play the economic association game?

I am utterly convinced that the economic association proposed by Quebec will be accepted. Remember that in order to defend itself against its neighbor, the American giant, Canada has always surrounded its markets with protective customs barriers. So American companies installed themselves within this barrier, especially in Ontario. Their production costs, however, remain sufficiently high for them to still need Canada's vast internal market. Ontario's natural sales market is Quebec, which represents between 30 per cent and 40 per cent of its market for certain manufactured goods. Giving up this market would mean the loss of thousands of jobs. Abolishing, in however small a way, the customs barriers with the United States would be to ruin the Ontario branches and subsidiaries of American companies. If Quebec makes a democratic decision to not make a complete break but to propose an association, I think that the other provinces will hear the voice of pragmatism and realism.

If Quebec eventually left Canada, would that not open the way for the political and economic break up of the Federation?

I am no prophet ... but two hypotheses are possible. First: that Canada will take advantage of the shock to reorganize itself, and I could very well see the creation of a group of semi-autonomous states, within a continuing Canadian dimension (in parallel with the association proposed by Quebec) but more flexible and larger. Such a reorganization would lead to a real decentralization of power in Canada, which is one of the most rigid, most over-administered, over-bureaucratized countries in the western world. Quebec has always been the eight-ball in the Federation, which is why lately they have preferred not to change the institutions, not to reorganize, in case Quebec should develop an appetite for more! This could be a good occasion on which to make a new thrust towards the future, which would enable everyone to breathe more easily and to breathe together. To my mind this is the first variation on the alternative open to Canada.

Second hypothesis: the "domino theory," which would be the traumatic ruin of a disintegrating Canada, with the Maritimes deciding to go it alone or choosing American protection, or even returning under the British umbrella, as the British tradition is very strong in those provinces, and Ontario trying desperately to maintain what remains. The West, which does not have the same Anglo-Saxon roots, would decide to join the United States. To me the idea is catastrophic; I do not want to consider it. English Canada has in fact enough tradition and enough "differences" in relation to the United States to want to maintain its own identity. ... Except perhaps in the prairie provinces around Alberta, but even there, there is still a preponderance of Anglo-British tradition ... notably the system of government which is that of the British Parliament rather than the American presidential system. We do have a tradition here. It is not for nothing that thousands of young Americans who justifiably contested certain aspects of the Vietnamese war found a hospitable land in Quebec, and elsewhere in Canada, and in Sweden. Many of them decided to remain, despite the pardon offered to them. Therefore there is enough of a Canadian identity, even though it has often remained fluid politically, even though the country stretches like a kind of permeable ribbon all along the American border. I therefore exclude this domino theory, in which the pieces fall one after the other, because Quebec withdrew its play. I am more confident than this and I think that our attitude, as time passes and the critical moment approaches, must be to try with all our powers to move in the direction of the first of our alternatives. We must remain very open to concerted action whatever happens, and despite any passing hostilities that might arise.

Do you foresee a separate currency and a central Quebec bank?

As you know this subject belongs in an area about which, as a whole, public opinion very easily becomes nervous. There is an aura almost of black magic to the word "monetary." First I must emphasize that Canadian monetary policy tends to do a disservice to the interests of eastern Canada, beginning with Quebec. As a result of distortion in the development of the country, when unemployment is being reabsorbed in Ontario, which is more developed than Quebec, our economy finds itself right in the hollow of the wave. In the event that Quebec one day becomes a sovereign state, the program of the Parti Québécois provides for the creation, at the start, of a bank which will give us control over the pulse of our financial institutions. This bank would be the government's financial agent.

But will there be a monetary union with Canada? Shall we in fact want to use the Canadian currency? My answer to these questions is yes. I, personally, am convinced that this will be right, and it is also one of the major elements of our plan for economic association with Canada. Looking at the European experiment, it would seem to be a difficult thing to realize. It is not simple. But unlike the old countries, we do not have that tradition of monetary sovereignty which is almost related to the national image, which makes the franc, the franc, and the lire, the lire. Here it is the contrary. There has been a currency common to the Canadian economic area, or common market, for a long time. One way and another it could be advantageous to retain this same standard provided that it is very closely watched in the area of equity and in the area of the sharing of obligations and constraints. To a large extent monetary independence is a fiction today. In a medium-scale economy, which is very open, very integrated with others and subject to the same external economic influence—that of the United States—the cost of the loss of monetary autonomy in comparison with political sovereignty is minimal. The more our economic objectives are similar, for instance with regard to inflation, the less important the loss of autonomy.

With some exceptions we want products, capital and people to continue to move, as far as possible, freely within the Canadian economic area. Why create impediments for individuals and for businesses by imposing at every point monetary constraints which would be to a large extent symbolic? We want to avoid the risk of fluctuations in the rate of exchange and, especially for business, the expense of converting money.

For us and for Canada it would therefore be advantageous to continue with our current monetary union.

In the 1960s, the Lesage government, of which you were a part, demanded economic emancipation for Quebec within the federal system. You are now demanding political emancipation, with very little emphasis on economic independence.

Jean Lesage talked a lot about economic emancipation, as I did at that time—this was in 1960. We are now at the end of the 1970s and things are very different. M. Lesage and I were then speaking within the context, accepted then, of a provincial state being part of federal Canada. Today the government of Quebec is talking from a perspective of anticipated political sovereignty—an important difference. Now any real economic emancipation must come through political sovereignty, as in fact our experiences in the '60s amply demonstrated! In 1962 when we launched the slogan: "Masters in our own home!" I was a little embarrassed. The basic issue was really only to regain control of electricity. It was a very good slogan, but I was well aware of the fact that recovering a certain number of electrical companies, even large ones, did not by a long stretch correspond with all the implications of "Masters in our own home!"

Today, as a result of my personal development, I know full well when I use that phrase that any talk of thrusting Quebec into the international field must take into account everything the slogan implies for what will follow.

Nothing must be left to chance. We must avoid intense trauma and errors in direction. It is fundamental at a time of a delicate transition that we safeguard the freedom of movement of people and of goods, which means the necessity for as close a customs union as possible. Our repeated proposals have never received any definite agreement. But no responsible politician outside Quebec has ever said that this union will not exist. We do not want to have to improvise. We always have in mind what could happen after the referendum if, as we hope, our option is approved, which is the immediate application of all the implications of the slogan: "Masters in our own home!" However we should not adopt tones of triumph now, which would be a little premature and presumptuous. This perhaps explains some of the slowness of which we are charged from time to time.

You have asked your services to calculate the exact cost and benefits of your membership in the Federation. Is this not a sign of your hesitation to leave the Federation?

The numbers are certainly useful, but for me they are of relative importance. Gray areas always exist when one is trying to assess the cost/benefit ratio of a political regime. It is almost impossible to determine the facts, and they would immediately be cut to pieces by contrary claims from the opposition. Example: A Canadian brigade forms part of the Atlantic forces stationed in Europe. Every taxpayer in Canada pays a portion of the cost. What is the exact cost? And how does Quebec benefit from this participation? It is impossible to put a value on this kind of operation.

But one fact emerges from the conclusions put forward by the experts: Quebec's membership in the federal regime has overall negative consequences for the province. Let us take a simple analogy. Imagine that I decide, in my day-to-day life, to give someone the responsibility of filling my refrigerator and I give him $50.00 for this purpose. Imagine again that this someone, with all the benefits of his great knowledge and wisdom, decides to send me, for example, a pretty stool, worth $50.00. This would not exactly correspond to my needs, but he could, however, tell me that I had indeed had my $50.00 worth.

This is what happens in many sectors in Quebec. We claim that the figures partially prove our argument. They show that that which Quebec has been able to give to the Federation has never been returned in the same proportion by federal policies which are fed, to a certain extent, by taxes raised in Quebec. We have given much, and during certain periods of our history when the province was lacking in awareness we gave in almost a servile fashion—as if it was inscribed that we should eternally allow our resources and our development to be syphoned elsewhere.

If we go back to the beginnings of the federal system we can find one particular case which magnificently illustrates this almost systematic "syphoning." Ontario consists of an area slightly smaller than Quebec. The railway network in Ontario, however, is much tighter, denser, more functional than in Quebec. This network helped to open up, and subsequently to serve the prairies and the west, . . . but, not to mince words, it has very often been more of a disservice to Quebec. Our province was the one that paid the most towards its construction because Quebec was the most heavily populated part of the country. We could say the same of our own times concerning the organization of air services. Quebec is under-serviced and presumably has been so, systematically. Despite this we pay our share, although we know perfectly well that our airports are less well organized and that our internal and external routes do not have adequate connections. The air transport situation in Quebec today resembles the railway situation in the nineteenth century. All this is part of the dispute which we have to sort out.

The air transport situation was aggravated by the air-traffic controllers' strike . . . .

The air-traffic controllers could not, and even now can obtain only with great difficulty, the right to communicate between each other in French! I am not talking about in the United States, or in the rest of Canada, but simply in Quebec. As with all cultural problems this question quickly became extremely emotional, but what had the most impression on me were the facts I learned during this conflict.

I learned, to my amazement, that the portion we paid to the federal Ministry of Transport amounted to almost 25 per cent of this ministry's budget—which is in proportion to the population of Quebec. Quebec, which is the largest province in Canada, possesses several international airports such as Mirabel, Dorval and Quebec. However, we found out that there are almost one thousand air-traffic controllers in western Ontario who control and direct, from Ontario, almost half of the territory of Quebec. On our other side, in New Brunswick, almost three hundred air-traffic controllers, for the most part grouped in Moncton which is a secondary airport, control from there all of eastern Quebec. The federal minister has allocated only two hundred air-traffic controllers to Quebec. This highly paid profession is extremely technological. It seems to have escaped Quebec.

Further, federal expenditures in Quebec which create jobs amount to only 14 or 15 per cent, approximately half the level of our participation. The proportions are the same for the salaries paid by Ottawa to Quebec francophone civil servants, who are very scarce among senior employees. The higher we climb towards the summit of the bureaucracy, the more we have recourse to very expensive personnel. It is at this level that our share is the least sufficient!

As far as the purchase of goods and services that a budget as enormous as the federal budget can inject into the economy is concerned, again we receive only 15 per cent—in other words more or less half of that to which we could normally lay claim. Equalization payments, the federal government's system of redistribution, in fact serves only to maintain the distortions rooted in the regime. We have over-developed Ontario and, as a whole, the Canadian west, while maintaining a state of relative underdevelopment in Quebec and in the Maritimes.

If Quebec becomes independent, it will have to carry many costs at present carried by the federal government . . . .

First, let us straighten up the idea of the magic dollars flowing from the federal purse! All this financial largesse is financed first and foremost by ourselves. We have to look at the whole in order to make any true estimate of the relationship between what we pay out and what we receive. For example: the pensions received by the proportion of Quebecers over sixty-five years of age does not entirely correspond with our input of almost 25 per cent of the federal budget. Elsewhere the opposite could be true. It is the grand total that counts. Each year we could save hundreds of millions of dollars spent on government bureaucracy. We often pay twice, at the provincial and at the federal level, for many services which tread on each others toes and which mutually render each other ineffective. The federal Minister of Agriculture very often follows policies which to us are undesirable and which sabotage the Quebec agricultural markets. This is the case very frequently in the milk industry, which is traditionally the backbone of Quebec agricultural production and which feels itself literally strangled. Other examples: the ministries of Forestry, those of Industry and Commerce, that of Social Welfare, and again in Ottawa, the Secretary of State responsible for the area covered by our minister of Cultural Affairs. Quebec pays its share, which is almost 25 per cent, for all these federal bodies but, given the differences in our societies and our desire to maintain the responsibility for that which belongs to us, we have also developed our own services in order to ensure the fulfillment of our needs.

In Ottawa a host of politicians—M. Trudeau is the most famous example—would stand guarantors of Canadian biculturalism. These people are francophones nominated to highly responsible posts by the federal power. Will this French power in Ottawa not hinder Quebec's progress towards sovereignty?

But Trudeau has failed. . . . He has failed on the major issues: failed in his economic policy; failed in certain presumptuous attitudes adopted towards some countries as if Canada could play at being a major power; failed in the matter of Canadian institutions and their adjustment to evolution. From the beginning everything was based on a vast ambiguity from which Trudeau could not extricate himself today and which is perfectly well illustrated by the expression—French power— which prevailed for so long. This power showed itself between 1967 and 1978 in the form of the "Three Wise Men." Marchand and Pelletier are now out of the arena. Their successors are men such as Lalonde and Chrétien whose "images" have not, nor have merited, the same impact. I think that we are witnessing the final tremors of this regime. Maybe they will survive one more ballot, but not more than that. We allowed to be created around these men the illusion of a power which would be the power of the minority which we are, a French power which would be constituted by the fact that the leader of the government, Trudeau, came from Quebec and his principal aides were also Quebec franco-phones. As a result Quebec would play a decisive role, which would perhaps be sufficient to alter the direction of Canada and make this country the binational, bicultural nation we have been dreaming of for so long. All this was revealed to be completely false. All that remains now is a law, the Official Languages Act, which P. E. Trudeau managed to force through, but literally by using blackmail. The Official Languages Act has changed nothing. Outside Quebec it has established only what we call "wicket bilingualism" which allows citizens to address a federal office, when they have the luck to find one, in French. The rest of Canada received this law badly; they found it difficult to swallow. When the government tried to extend its application to federal civil servants, the reaction of the Ottawa mandarins was literally poisonous, with the result that the Trudeau government suffered a number of serious losses in by-elections both in the federal capital and in several surrounding areas, and these losses were partly due to the peevishness of anglophone federal civil servants who could not tolerate the biculturali-zation of the federal public service.

Our November 1976 victory gave a certain new lease on life to Trudeau and his government. He may indeed win another election, as if he were the last insurance against what many Anglo-Canadians consider to be the danger that we represent. Just as in 1968, they may think that it is absolutely necessary to elect a Quebecer to best fight against another Quebecer. The fact remains, however, that Trudeau's failure has helped us by enabling us to find out how illusory the so-called French power was.

Do the results of the last by-elections, and Trudeau's losses confirm what you have just said?

Well, the pendulum was barely primed for a return swing, . . . but now we can see very precisely just how it is moving outside Quebec. I am no prophet. I remember that in 1958 (it is strange how this works in ten-year cycles) we had the "vision of the North," then Diefenbaker's great success, almost the Diefenbaker wave. We know how that died. It took longer in the case of what was called Trudeaumania, in 1968. . . . At that time a number of people told me: "Trudeau is something of an empty vessel." In other words he is the vessel for those who are discontented, and frustrated, and also for those who, though they do not say so, would like Quebec to cease to evolve. Into the vessel—Trudeau—everyone threw their prejudices, their wild hopes, their boredom, because there was really little there other than a kind of "glamor" campaign to sell an image: Trudeaumania. Today, obviously, the pendulum has swung the other way. It is inevitable. Remember also that, over and above the Trudeau factor, the Liberal party has been in power in Ottawa for fifteen years. It is like a lease. It is normal for it to run out. In addition, the party has had the same figurehead for more than ten years, who arrived in a wave of frenzy that nothing could have satisfied, or maintained indefinitely.

I find this government's economic management completely unrealistic. Down in Ottawa they have control over the most enormous budgetary resources—over taxes—but also over tariffs, i.e., over foreign exchange. And over monetary policy which is in effect a kind of regulator of all that. I think I must say that, as "mismanagers", if they have not won the championship, they are very close. I do not know what will happen at the next federal elections, but one thing is for sure: we are witnessing the end of an era. Will it come after indeterminate elections? Will there be a minority government? Obviously this cannot go on indefinitely. It is as simple as that. It is the law of nature.

He seems to have been rejected by the anglophones. Only Quebec keeps him in power . . . .

We are not at the elections yet. Do not underestimate the resources of an extraordinarily opportunist party which, when it has found itself in trouble, has always tried to make spectacular about-turns and recoveries. Do not underestimate the power of attachment to power, perhaps more so in the case of the Liberal party than in any other, because it comprises such an assortment of interests. It has no doctrine; it does not even have anything which could claim to be the basis of a doctrine.

As for Quebec, I have the impression that this is the usual situation. It was true for Laurier, it was true for Saint-Laurent. And I think we could say the same for Diefenbaker; he comes from Saskatchewan and Saskatchewan stayed with him federally even in defeat. Today, Saskatchewan is still Conservative. There is a sort of durable solidarity which persists around the memory of this old man who, to the people of the west, is one of them. The same is true in Quebec. We are not inclined to destroy one of our own people because we consider that, in a sense, this makes us a little weaker. So, just as it was true for Laurier, and for Saint-Laurent, I have the feeling that it will also be true to a large extent for the Liberals in Quebec as long as Trudeau is there. But this will not prevent the rest of the country from moving in the opposite direction.

When you announced that the referendum was a mandate to negotiate, did you not take away from Trudeau ammunition for his next electoral campaign?
I hope so! because he is still wearing the very artificial coat of the savior of federalism. He treats us as a "particle" but we are a party, and we are in power. He said we were dead and buried, but the people he buried are looking pretty good on the whole! This is not a case of dramatization; it is not a case of fighting against him directly. It is simply a case of letting

him come to terms with his problems. We do not have to provide him with any special ammunition. What we have been saying for the past two or three months has nothing to do with Trudeau, either directly or indirectly. It was conceived neither to contribute to his defeat, nor to keep him in power. It is the principle that is important, not the asides. Within this context the future of federal politicians, whether they be Trudeau, Clark or whoever (I am going to use a term here which he has already used for the Quebec premiers), the future of these people is something of an ephiphenomenon. This is true as far as the principle of the question is concerned. It is true for any man too, to a certain point, unless he takes himself to be several others at the same time!

Marc Lalonde has declared that Quebec should not expect economic co-operation from the rest of Canada should it decide to separate.

Poor Lalonde! He published two studies recently: one on sovereignty-association which is important for the number of contradictions he attributes to us, and another on the economy. In both cases he was obliged—and this is a sensational change—to discuss our cause and even to mention it by name in the titles: sovereignty-association. This would have been unthinkable a year ago. It shows just to what point things have evolved: they have to discuss it now. Obviously, however, they have to arrive at a negative conclusion. Put yourself in their place—they are defending the bulwark of the *status quo*. In addition to this there is a certain David Crombie, a not unremarkable man and a new force in politics, who has just been elected from Toronto. He was the one, essentially, who brought about the licking of the Liberals by the Conservatives. I read something that Crombie said, at the risk of being wrongly interpreted because it was right in the middle of the electoral campaign, at the end of September. The substance of his words was: "When I hear people like Davis"—or it could be Lalonde or anyone else"—

reply to a man who wishes eventually to negotiate: 'I will
never negotiate!,' I do not understand what they mean. . . . It
is basically so stupid that I do not understand." And
furthermore he is not the only person to have said that if
Quebec makes a definite decision to negotiate on the basis of a
new option, it will be necessary at least to talk about it and to
negotiate. Now that is either the reaction of an intelligent
man or else the reaction of a man whom politics has not yet
fixed in his attitudes. But this is what will happen. There was
a time when it was said that "The queen does not negotiate
with her subjects." When politicians say *never*, one should be
suspicious—because the queen negotiates fully with her
subjects. In history there have continually been errors of this
kind, and history is also full of men like Lalonde or others who
say: "Never!" It is always the same. And afterwards? We are
not in such a great hurry. It may take two years, or four years,
or five years if necessary—but I do not think it will take more
than four or five years. In any case, things are moving in this
direction. There is a current running throughout the world
which is the same as the most obvious current of evolution in
Quebec. Furthermore it is in the interest, both political and
economic, of Canada—so, why not?

*What should we think about the threat of a counter-referendum, which
Trudeau has indicated that he will hold across Canada if ever Quebec
replied "yes"?*

They can have as many referendums as they like, but on one
condition: that they do not imagine (we saw what happened
over the question of conscription, for example) that they are
going to make Quebecers oppose each other, that they are
going to make the rest of Canada oppose Quebec, and that
they are going to achieve valid results. If they ever do this
they will only bring about the break that we want to avoid.
We do not want a breach: we want the readaptation of two
societies, a coexistence which would allow them both to

breathe in their own ways, while enabling them to continue to co-operate both politically and economically in essential areas to their mutual advantage. If they try to oppose the opinion of Quebec—though no one wanted to twist Newfoundland's arm when Newfoundland called a referendum in order to decide upon its future—if they try to oppose it with a referendum in the rest of the country which were to say "I do not agree", at that moment they would be running headlong towards a break. In any case it would not have any real effect on what happened subsequently, because as Quebec's wish to negotiate something new with the rest of the country became more clear, and as the time came closer, the negative and sterile common front which men like Trudeau and Lalonde try to maintain would collapse in people's minds. For this reason Quebec's "yes", despite the fact that some people are forever afraid of its being watered down, will have decisive weight.

One has the impression that the political parties opposing you will conduct very tough campaigns. . . . There is already evidence of this.

We do not expect anyone to make us a gift of victory! We know very well that they have the weight of money behind them, but the weight of money is subject to the law of diminishing returns. . . . One cannot conduct indefinite orgies; one can do it for a certain length of time only, but no longer. At the time of the referendum, as during the elections, the law states that expenses should be strictly controlled. The rest of their arguments are the arguments of fear. And fear is also subject to diminishing returns. . . . In 1970 they said: "No to separation, no to the separatists!", in 1973 they said: "No to separation, no to separatists!", in 1976 they said: "No to separation, no to separatists!" This has not hindered our progress.

Do you think that really applied in 1973?

Certainly it applied! But our vote increased from 23 per cent to 31 per cent. They took one constituency away from us, but what mattered (it took us time to realize this because it is hard to lose one constituency when one holds only seven) was to see the popular vote increase from 23 per cent to 31 per cent. This is, after all, the important result. So much the better if we had won additional constituencies. If I were obliged to choose between a lowering of the popular vote and an increasing number of constituencies, in the context of a people who would have to decide on their future, I would immediately choose an increase in the popular vote. ... So much the better if one has additional constituencies.

What will happen to supporters of the status quo or of a revised federal system if your option is eventually approved by a majority of Quebecers?

Let us go back to the American example. A certain number of American loyalists who remained faithful to the British crown left the United States after Independence to settle in Canada, England or elsewhere. They were the founders of what is now known as Ontario, and of the territory to the east of Quebec, i.e., New Brunswick, and they helped to colonize part of Quebec, in the eastern counties. Several thousand Americans left the United States as a result of fundamental intellectual disagreement on the future of the country. The same sort of exodus, smaller, and less dramatic, could occur. It will certainly happen to several hundreds, perhaps several thousands, of Quebecers, including francophones, who will not accept the decision of the majority if it is in our direction. It is not surprising that all those who profit from the present regime should fight to continue to profit from it. There are also Quebecers who are fundamentally convinced that it would be better to maintain the *status quo* than to change the regime. This conviction, which has nothing to do with interests, is infinitely respectable, and our role is to attempt to convert these people without aggression.

PART 4

❀

The Referendum

During your last electoral campaign in 1976 you promised that, if you succeeded, you would organize a referendum on the constitutional future of the province. Two years have passed since you took power. It is now said that the referendum will not take place in the spring of 1979, but in 1980.

We decided, and we announced, and we stand by our announcement, that the central referendum on the question will take place during the mandate of this legislature. Our mandate may last the legal limit of five years, that is to say until autumn, 1981, but tradition demands that it should last for approximately four years. We cannot yet say what date the referendum will be held, but incertitude in this respect does not prevent all those who wish to work either for or against our option from doing so from this moment onwards. They have nothing to lose.

During the electoral campaign the P.Q. never said that victory in the November 15 elections would lead to an immediate proclamation of independence. Quebecers have been aware of this since 1974, when the National Executive and the parliamentary caucus of party adopted a so-called stage-by-stage policy.

Quebec has never before drafted a law on the subject of a referendum. So we had to prepare one after studying what had been done elsewhere, notably in Newfoundland, where the people were consulted on two occasions prior to the entry of Newfoundland into the Confederation. We also studied the case of England when it entered the Common Market, the Swiss cantons, and France. The law is now ready, and henceforth the referendum procedure can be put into gear at any time.

I never minimized the question of "separation" during

the 1976 campaign. It is no secret that the fundamental aim of the P.Q. is to achieve sovereignty, which is the only way to obtain the equality of two peoples, cultural security for our people, regional equilibrium, and to put an end to manipulation from outside. To a large extent we have breached the process of Quebec's participation in the Canadian federal regime. Our strategy now provides that we will soon open up the most positive and most exciting stage of the campaign which will lead to the referendum, which will be the first chance that history has given to Quebecers to decide, themselves, on their collective future.

Why did you prepare a White Paper which resulted in a draft law on referendum in Quebec?

The White Paper was not a bill in the strictly juridical sense. It was essentially a statement of what would be contained in the bill. We followed the British tradition, using a system of White Papers which in fact start out as Green Papers, which establish some perspectives within a given area. The White Paper on the referendum was very concise, very concrete, very compact, in order that it would be very clear, and it philosophized as little as possible. It simply established the principle of the right to have recourse to public consultation. It evoked the theory of popular initiative which we would like to see develop in Quebec as a political practice. Principally, however, it laid out the form that a consultation initiated by the government, which is to say, a referendum, would take. After an interminable number of debates, the law finally came into force in June 1978.

Suppose that 50 per cent of Quebecers vote yes in the referendum and therefore give you a mandate to negotiate. Taking into account the fact that almost 20 per cent of Quebec are anglophone, would this percentage in fact indicate the agreement of a net majority of Quebecers?

Indeed it would, if 50 per cent plus one vote "yes!" There is one point, however. If the anglophone minority which represents 18 to 20 per cent of the vote were to declare massively against, even if we were to carry only 50 or 51 per cent of the votes, this would clearly indicate a very strong majority among the francophone population. But let us leave this referendum arithmetic to one side for a while. What is happening in the minds of Quebecers? Certainly time is working on our side. Barely ten years ago only people under thirty-five favored the "independentist" idea. The vast majority of those over forty supported the federalists. Today, by means of regular polls, we calculate that the younger generation of 1968 has abandoned none of its early convictions and that the young people of 1978 are, as a whole, even more instinctively, *québécois*. English Canada should no longer imagine that it can revert to the pressures it imposed in an earlier period and keep Quebec "under a bushel." The national sentiment of Quebecers is a reality, and if anglophone Canada were to persist in trying to stifle it, we would quickly see the development of a more radical nationalism.

Supposing you get 48 per cent, for example . . . .

I almost prefer not to think about that. . . . It would be somewhat dangerous . . . because any figure around the 45-50 per cent mark obviously signifies that the majority of francophones voted yes. I would prefer the francophone majority (with a certain number of anglophones, because there are some—especially among the young—who support us) to completely carry a yes vote. If not it would be, shall we say, difficult to swallow. It would mean that a francophone majority had clearly expressed a "yes", but that they had been blocked by a minority. And even if those are the rules of the game. . . . It is for this reason that we will work our feet off in order to have 50 per cent or over.

When you announced that the referendum would give you a mandate to negotiate, were you thinking that this would give you a greater chance of obtaining a yes majority?

No, because the majority of our opponents will never agree with us. Most of them, obviously, are anglo-Quebecers, who instinctively prefer to remain with the "Canadian" majority, the majority of the rest of the country. There are certainly some ideologically committed political opponents also, and then in addition all those who perhaps share a few negative opinions. Which all proves, whatever anyone might think, the importance of the referendum. We must divest ourselves of whatever complex it is that makes us believe that our voice does not have much weight. It is a question of negotiating, is it not? It is a question of a mandate to negotiate sovereignty and association or, in other words, the means of putting to an end the federal regime as far as it relates to Quebec? Let us not have any illusions about this: though it is only a mandate to negotiate, it is nonetheless an historic and decisive mandate from the point of view of change. It is not for nothing that they are working, and will continue to work for a "no". But it is the "yes" which will decide the question.

Some people maintain that sovereignty is not negotiable.

We must put a stop to this nonsense. This kind of statement is just a play on words. It is obvious that in a certain sense sovereignty is not negotiable. If Quebec expresses its wish to be a sovereign state (even if it does so within a framework of negotiation, because we do accept that certain things must continue and that there must be association between the two peoples), what we negotiate beyond that will essentially be association. But if we negotiate association, by definition we will achieve sovereignty. We have already stated what the three essential points of association will be. The two which concern Quebec and Canada are the market and the currency.

But at the same time, if we begin to negotiate, and if negotiation continues, although we are not negotiating sovereignty, we certainly have to negotiate the repatriation of powers because this is not something that will be done overnight. . . . Our party program states that we will demand that power be repatriated. And "demand" is a pleasantly resounding word. However, whether we say we "demand," or whether we say we "will look for," by definition we imply that there will be negotiation on a number of issues, such as transfers and timing, etc. One cannot build a complete national government overnight, and for this reason we must negotiate.

If there are instruments for some form of economic association, does that suppose, as M. Morin has already suggested, some sort of parliament, or of representation?

No, not at all. Furthermore, as if often the case with those wretched headlines which are arranged to try and create news, they were unfair. (When there isn't enough news in the content of a story they make it with the headlines. It is the current sickness of the news media. . . . The news is therefore becoming much more spectacular than thirty years ago, but I really feel that at the same time, the fundamental integrity of information, its fundamental honesty, is taking a beating.) So if you read the headlines on the subject of Claude Morin it is one thing; if you read the content it is another. If I remember correctly, M. Morin, who was already noted as a teacher, was called upon to give two or three lectures at Sherbrooke University. At one particular moment he was asked about models of associations in the world. As there are all sorts of models, he explained a number of them, including the European one which is moving towards the election of a multinational parliament, and it was following this that someone clever decided that perhaps the headline should be on the possibility of a parliament, in other words of a new federal parliament. I find this need to create news . . . a little difficult to digest. In fact there will eventually have to be bodies which, at least at the technocratic level, will have to be formed to administer common areas. In other words there will certainly be secretariats to administer agreements on markets and an agreement on currency. We will need administrative structures for this. We will also need ministers responsible for these areas, on both sides, who would meet a few times a year. There could also be a delegated parliament, to which both sides would delegate members who are already elected to their parliaments, and which would meet once or twice a year—which is what has been happening so far in Europe. It could go further if necessary, but on one condition: that, when the time comes, sovereignty in all its defined dimensions is neither affected nor restricted by exterior structures.

Still within this same context, how do you view M. Ryan's arrival on the scene?

Let me say one thing which I have never said before, except to a few of our friends when the Liberal party congress was in progress. It is true that, overall, Ryan can give some sort of reformist image, some sort of image of integrity. He has never had to fight in politics, so it was perhaps easier to give himself an image of this kind. That said, the person I most preferred to see as leader of the Liberal party and as an opponent was M. Ryan. I have the impression that certain of his weaknesses—everyone has some—will appear soon enough and that his political efficacy will not be as great as some imaginative minds were blowing it up out of all measure to be. Furthermore the integrity, or at least the image of integrity, which he has brought is also useful for society as a whole. Therefore on the two levels he was the person I most wanted to see in this position. Only the future will tell what will happen. I noticed one thing that he said, in that slightly underhand way he has of taking indirect shots at his opponents to see if there is some way of undermining them without naming them directly. He said (I am not quoting exactly, but more or less): "It is perhaps better that I have reached this position at the age of fifty-three, rather than thirty or thirty-five, which would have been too soon." I do not know at whom this was aimed; I, myself, entered politics at thirty-seven. Everyone has his moment in life. . . . However I am not sure that his reasoning is sound, because at his age it is difficult to discard certain of the habits one has acquired . . . a certain pontifical style for example, and things which have become completely engrained over the course of the years. It is hard to discard this and try to reacquire some measure of flexibility. Muscles in the figurative as well as the physical sense, harden with age. I wish ill to no one, but I have the feeling that, once again on all levels, he is the best opponent we could have.

It has been said that Ryan's arrival was a step backwards, towards Duplessism.

No, no, I think we must be fair. I think Ryan is man who, by means of many pilgrimages, sometimes very laborious like his columns in *Le Devoir* with all that implies by way of research, has aimed to keep himself up to date. But between keeping oneself up to date on information from the outside, and plunging into this very difficult jungle of an active political life, there is one hell of a leap. I have the impression that with all his qualities and all his faults, M. Ryan is beginning to regain a very normal stature. A party congress idealizes, and it inflates one's image terribly. But I think people are aware that, after all, he is just an ordinary man, one among many, just as I am, just as the others are. Messiahs . . . there are none.

Pierre Elliott Trudeau promised, in December 1976, to resign if Quebecers voted for independence. If you lose the referendum will you do likewise?

I replied at the time that I would make no such frivolous promises. Let Trudeau feel free to dramatize the situation. However, in one sense the federal Prime Minister was drawing a logical conclusion: to a large extent does he not owe his re-election since 1968 to the fact that the anglophones consider him the only politician capable of preventing Quebec's withdrawal from the confederation? As far as I am concerned I have no intention of resigning if the response to the referendum is unfavorable. We were elected to replace Robert Bourassa and to provide a "real government" for Quebec. Our mandate is not linked to the result of the referendum which, during the whole campaign, we carefully distinguished from good economic and political administration.

The entry of Newfoundland into the Federation was decided in two referendums. Do you think Quebec's exit from the Federation could occur as a result of a referendum open to Quebecers only?

This referendum will involve Quebecers only. Any intervention, federal or otherwise, would be rejected as a manifestation of insupportable tutelage. I cannot say anything yet about the proceedings which would follow a favorable result. I remember during my official visit to Paris in November 1977 saying: "It is becoming more and more likely that a new country will appear, through the democratic process, on the map." I know that some great minds have proposed that a counter-referendum, organized by Ottawa, should be held to "correct" the results of the one we are going to organize. Trudeau even announced one day, in a somewhat impromptu fashion, that his government was considering national consultation. Furthermore he shortly afterwards proposed a bill to this effect. But his improvised text is full both of so many holes and so many excesses that it is difficult to take it seriously. It is at the most an instrument of blackmail for a regime on its last legs.

In your opinion will it be necessary for there to be several referendums in order for the Quebec option to triumph?

I formally exclude the possibility of a second referendum during the same mandate. Furthermore our law forbids this. For the rest, we cannot be sure. Trudeau and other politicians have suggested holding a torrent of referendums, doubltess in order to try and ridicule the one we promised to hold before the end of this legislature. There is a precedent for this, here in Canada. The province of Newfoundland was the only one to be democratically consulted over its entry into Confederation. The others were more or less thrown into Confederation and only consulted later by this regime which, despite being one of the oldest in the world, is no less imperial and colonial by birth. The inhabitants of Newfoundland were consulted twice. The first time, in 1948, three questions were posed: they were asked either to conserve their traditional link with the British crown (because they were under the administration of the crown in London), or to become totally autonomous, or finally to join with Canada. The first consultation eliminated right away the possibility of maintaining direct dependence on London. Of the two other options, neither prevailed. A second referendum which was organized eighteen months later, in 1949, proposed two alternative solutions: either self-government, or joining with Canada. The federal link won by a slender majority. The precedent exists.

But Ottawa could refuse to take into account the result of the referendum. There is no shortage of historical examples of referendums and plebiscites which have not been recognized and which have even served as a pretext for forceful intervention. The premier of Saskatchewan has not dismissed the possibility of catastrophic consequences should Quebec declare its independence.

Each time such consultations have produced a clear decision, the results have imposed themselves of their own accord. People have refused to recognize the inferences when plebiscites or referendums have been held within a context of coercion. I can see no sign of this in Quebec. One can never be completely sheltered from errors on the way, but I think that Canadian democracy and the responsible attitudes often manifested in English Canada and in Quebec are a form of guarantee. If the Quebec people, very clearly and very democratically, indicate their will to change, including their wish for sovereignty, the rest of Canada will not be able to do other than accept this collective decision without losing their honor.

Contrary to certain allegations, Quebecers do not consider their anglophone minority to be a community of hostages. On the contrary, this is the richest social group, occupying the highest posts in the economy, in finance, and in private enterprise. If they were to admit that they had ever thought of it, the federal authorities could not justify intervention in Quebec such as they carried out in 1970 after the kidnapping of James Cross and Pierre Laporte, on the pretext either of conspiracy or of attempted insurrection.

What would you do if Ottawa refused to open its doors to negotiation to define the new relationship between Quebec and the rest of Canada? These links of interdependence which you have offered, in advance, on several occasions seem to have been offered in vain, as the provincial premiers have categorically refused them.

In my opinion simple good sense, based on our geopolitical situation, excludes the possibility of the door being shut once and for all. And I do not think that the time involved will be very great. Basically the anglophone majority in Canada behaves in a rather patronizing way, which is normal after two centuries of domination. For my part I know of no master, especially one with "divine right," well anchored in absolute certitudes, who would not answer his employees presenting claims for the first time that he refused to negotiate, and who would destroy his business rather than give in. When the time comes the master, if he still has a head on his shoulders, will forget the idea of turning the key in the door and will negotiate, knowing that he has some interests to guard for the future. Absolute refusals, categorical declarations made *ex-cathedra*, the "We will never accepts" which have been pronounced by a number of politicians, are founded on a simplistic strategy which is once again to make the frightened, nervous minority, which we were until November 15, 1976, tremble and hesitate. During the last election campaign our Liberal opponents and the entire battery of the financial circles, which are the vassals of the current federal regime, tried as hard as possible to ruin us by means of abusive propaganda in which the key phrase: "No to separatism, it would be the end of the world" was repeated endlessly with all the evocations of an apocalypse which they could brandish with which to frighten us. Such exploitation of the conceivable outcome of a break with the *status quo* is traditional, but the clamoring and the campaign of false alarms were subject to the law of diminishing returns.

The rumor of the moving of corporate head offices out of Montreal was a panic reaction. Brought down to more equitable proportions, what do we find? That companies are opening in Toronto or Calgary (as others in the United States left New York for Chicago); that they are moving into new areas of development, towards the west and Alberta, and not fleeing some sort of appalling "Quebecization" of our economy. That said, however, we do expect predictions of catastrophe to continue to increase during this period of reassessment which opened with our accession to power.

Supporters of federalism accuse you of not having waited for the verdict of Quebecers in the referendum, and of having largely initiated a systematic process of nibbling at Ottawa's power. When the referendum happens, your adversaries are saying that it will by then be too late.

I promised to play the game and to govern Quebec according to the existing rules, as a Canadian province, and not as a prefiguration of the sovereign state of Quebec. But the rule of rules in this system of phony Confederation which is, in reality, a true federation in which Ottawa encroaches on all provincial powers, is to continually and vigorously fight against the federal power. We must regain control of our immigration policy, of our language and communications policies (television, radio, broadcasting), of our natural resources, of our savings, to mention only the most pressing. We do not have the right to wait until the end of our long march before trying, as all our predecessors in the federal-provincial tug-of-war have done, whether we do so in vain or not, to repatriate for the benefit of Quebecers all those elements necessary for their survival and their development.

You have adopted Law 101 on the francisation of Quebec. Other laws have been, or will be voted, which will make profound changes to the province in the areas of cultural development, control of natural resources, and the financing of the parties. What remains for the referendum once so many thorny issues have been resolved?

Everything will remain because a change in its political status is fundamental to a society. It seems to me to be perfectly normal that we should work on some aspects on our way towards to the referendum. Let us take as an example the case you cited, which was the most dramatic event of the first parliamentary session in which we were the majority party. This is not a case of conscious and planned surreptitious imposition of the sovereignty-association option. We were thrust into this language problem by ten years of precedents. You will recall that the problem took a turn for the worse in 1966. At that time, I remember, I was a member in the National Assembly on the opposition benches. This was in the months following the defeat of the Lesage government of which I had been a member. All at once two factors seemed to connect in the collective perception, which suddenly precipitated everything. The first factor was the birth rate which had been declining dramatically for some years. The second was the galloping assimilation of immigrants by the anglophone minority. It was at this time that Quebec opened a Ministry of Immigration to try and find some sort of answer to the question, which we all knew was extremely important. However, fundamental power in that area still remains in federal hands.

What do you intend to do about the problems of immigration?

Immigration must be closely watched by the community as a whole. This is vital for us. Currently, but this has also traditionally been the case over the last hundred years, the federal government which represents an anglophone majority is pursuing in a slightly less overt fashion than in the past an immigration policy which is based on the maintenance of an anglophone majority and as far as possible a majority of immigrants with Anglo-Saxon roots. For generations, at the expense of everyone, including Quebecers, the federal government has maintained a very active network of immigration offices in England, Scotland and Ireland, while there has never been one in France. Sovereignty means having, in these sectors, the power normal to a national community which administers its own affairs itself, as a function of its own future.

On the thorny and emotional question of language would it not be preferable to wait for the verdict of the referendum? Instead you have made a war-horse of the issue since you took power. Discussions on Law 101, which took many long and precious months at the beginning of your mandate, monopolized the attention and the energy of the whole of Quebec.

We do not believe that a birth policy could, alone, resolve the problem of the decreasing number of francophones in Quebec. We assessed this from one sign. As I have said, at the same time that the birth rate was decreasing the assimilation of immigrants, those whom we currently call New Canadians, or New Quebecers, increased dramatically. Approximately nine out of every ten immigrants disembarking in Quebec joined the anglophone community. I do not mean the anglophone community of the whole of Canada, but just that of Quebec. Our perception of this situation and of the upsets and the reaction it provoked in our society made us consider the matter as a cultural problem. We found ourselves suddenly exposed to becoming less numerous every day and one day, who knows, perhaps in the minority. Fairly serious incidents broke out in the region of Montreal, where questions of language and of assimilation have always been posed with more acuity than elsewhere. Ten years later we still talk about the incidents in Saint-Léonard which is approximately 50 per cent Italian and 50 per cent francophone. Movements favoring the integration of the schools began to appear. I did not agree with their radicalism. A series of bills tried to attack the problem from the angle of linguistic policy. Bill 63 was voted, but was rejected unanimously—it was, indeed, a spineless law. Subsequently Law 85 was aborted. Finally Robert Bourassa arrived. During his years in power he was the artisan of Law 22, which was also considered a disgrace by a great number of the francophone society, perhaps with some exaggeration. During the last electoral campaign, as a result of disruptions which had occurred in Robert Bourassa's entourage and among the Liberals, and following a series of improvisations made in the midst of the campaign, the Parti Québécois was led to promise to do something. The situation could not be allowed to go on any longer. . . . During a first "hole-stopping" session which took place before the end of 1976, barely a month after our arrival in power, we had to take on a commitment to resolve the language question. Several distressing cases had arisen in the schools. A kind of minority confrontation was organizing, mustering together several small political groups. Therefore ten years of discord and failed attempts literally forced us into the position of having to vote Law 101. Quebecers reject the fact that speaking French in their own country should be a handicap in their professional life or an impediment to their participation in the Canadian world. But this is precisely what they were reminded during their conflict with pilots of Canadian airplanes, who refused to use French in conversation with the control towers of Quebec airports.

When the debate on Law 101 on the language was closed, you gave the impression of not being completely satisfied. . . .

Yes, I regret that people thought that our action in this area was planned with a view to persuading Quebecers to be more favorably disposed towards the referendum. This problem is ten years old and has been the subject of the efforts of three legislatures. As a result of the suspicions, as a result of the deep gulf existing in Quebec between the anglophone minority and the francophone majority, discussions within the country and in the Assembly were conducted in a manner which I find still, today, extremely distressing. All the anglophone establishment and all the forces opposing Law 101 voted against us in November 1976. Now the law has increasingly hardened their position against us and the gap between us and the anglophones has widened. Our only comfort after three fruitless attempts is that for the first time a language law seems, in essence, to have fulfilled the aspirations of the majority, i.e., the French people of Quebec.

We have not seen any of the counter-demonstrations, any of the bitterness, or any of the explosions which occurred when the preceding laws were adopted.

As far as the debate is concerned, it is obvious that everything which, either closely or at a distance, touches on the problem of language involves a very emotional area. Even more so in a country such as ours where two population blocs have always lived more or less like two hermits within the same house and where, in addition, one of the blocs claims to be victimized. I personally consider this to be a mistaken view. We uphold the privileges and rights—more than for any other minority in the world—of our anglophone citizens. However, the anglophones felt themselves victimized and this feeling took a disagreeable, even a bitter turn. Now the results seem to auger well for the future, but it is only with time that we will really find out. Within the provincial context, in any case, the question has been resolved as was necessary. One of the reasons I have dreamed of political sovereignty is precisely so that we will not have to legislate on questions which should be as clear as the air we breathe. The language of a people and their rights to use it should not be protected by a fortress of laws, but until there is a new order of things, we are obliged to follow this route.

This is a law which, in practice, forces the use of the French language, and which corners the federal power of Ottawa . . . .

The linguistic question as posed, especially in the areas of teaching, business, and the administration (the three areas covered by the law) in our opinion in no way challenges the federal regime in Ottawa. It is part of that sector of competence which already falls under the provincial jurisdiction. That being said, we should not ignore the fact that the present government has to do at least as much as the governments which preceded it to maintain or enlarge its own areas of competence. It seems to me that this occurs in all federal regimes where there is confrontation of this kind between the federal government and state or provincial governments, and that the general phenomenon is even more apparent when there are two cultural entities involved, each with its own perception of its own identity and its own national conscience. The Province of Quebec is isolated within nine provinces which are solidly and eternally anglophone. Even in New Brunswick, which has the largest francophone minority, the proportion is only 35 per cent of the population. Quebec is the only province which faces a federal government which it can never control because the majority—by which I mean the anglophone majority— determines the decisions made by the federal government. It is therefore inevitable in the time between now and the referendum that there will be moments when we will argue on specific points. But everything will be resolved on the great occasion of the referendum.

In sum, you have adopted Gerald Godin's formula: "Let us try to diversify the sources of our independence." But in trying to negotiate step by step you are increasingly worrying those who want to move quickly towards "operation-truth," i.e., the referendum.

We are trying both to maintain and to enlarge the competence of the provincial government, without encroaching on our future program. Obviously we cannot consider allowing a good opportunity for confrontation to pass if it presents itself . . . and God knows, there are many! But we will not break the rules of the democratic game! Suppose the result of the referendum is negative vis-a-vis our option. We would therefore remain provincial for a certain number of years. And I promise you that we would not forgive ourselves for not having increased as far as possible the opportunities for maintaining or developing the powers of Quebec.

But in the end will the federal government in Ottawa not fight back?

Oh, it fights as it fights! It moves fairly jumpily—even irrationally. It multiplies its committees so well that you need a guide to find your way around them! I think that the Liberals are still suffering the effects of an element of disequilibrium. The victory of the P.Q. was traumatic for them. But I suppose that they will organize themselves properly as the due date approaches and that they will do legitimately what is necessary to defend the regime they believe in. Beyond the question of the language which is already in the realm of provincial competence, on the basis of the present rules of the game there remains first and foremost to change the fact that the *largest* part, the most strategic part of the taxes we pay, goes to Ottawa to fill the purse of a government which primarily reflects the needs of the nine anglophone provinces. Certainly this majority is not necessarily opposed to us but it almost always, logically, serves itself first . . . in order to ensure its development. Will our taxes continue for much longer to enrich another government, or will they remain with us? And our financial institutions founded on our Caisses Populaires, the local tradition, represented by the savings banks, the chartered banks, our insurance companies which, with the pension funds, are among the largest reservoirs of accumulated capital, will these also continue for much longer to be manipulated so easily from outside our territory? And the credit which results, and the savings which accumulate, and the capital; will they continue to be formed under federal administration and federal legislation, which allows them to be invested in a manner so detrimental to the development of Quebec? After the referendum we will have to ensure, as Canada was able to do in its time, that we can establish regulations in Quebec which will enable us to channel our capital and our savings towards ourselves, in order that they can serve towards the effective development of Quebec. "What is sauce for the goose is sauce for gander," goes the old English proverb.

We will also have to maintain our demographic equilibrium, a factor which could always elude us, at least partially, under the present regime. And will we one day have the right, which is normal to a nation, without being manipulated and controlled by the federal government, to be able to conduct relations as we please with whom we please elsewhere in the world, as a function of our natural proclivities and our own interests? Or shall we continue to have international relations which are charted, restricted and often bedevilled by the power of the state which rests in federal hands?

Many anglophone immigrants recall that they chose Canada as their new country, despite the fact that they settled in Quebec. They are now complaining that you are suddenly changing the rules of the game by ensuring the predominance of the French language.

Even the Bourassa government, which was particularly orthodox as far as the *status quo,* the collective institutions, was concerned legislated in its own fashion on the language. Law 22 changed the rules of the traditional game by establishing certain safeguards against the galloping assimilation of immigrants into the anglophone community. Never was Bourassa suspected of wanting to change the rules of the game! But our political option provokes sinister apprehensions each time we make any sort of move.... The example of the Italians, who adapt very quickly to our society, is interesting in this respect. Two waves of immigration followed one after the other. The prewar wave was assimilated into French society in Quebec. After the war, as a result of the sort of "continentalism" which over a period of thirty or thirty-five years tended to dwarf French Quebec, the Quebec Italians turned towards our anglophone neighbors. But this is a situation which could be changed around once again through the exercise of our sovereignty. With Law 101 there will no longer be any confusion possible for foreigners arriving in Quebec. They will know that it is a country which is officially French-speaking. They will know that French is the language of work, and the administrative language. Those who arrive will know that they will have to adapt as well as possible to this society. We will put an end to the ambiguity which has lasted for too long of *la Belle province*, which although French, is at the same time part of English Canada.

PART 5

❧

A Feeling of Urgency

Was the arrival in power of the P.Q. not considered a "swing to the left" by Quebec?

In Anglo-Canadian business circles, the question of sovereignty provokes an emotive response without fail. This is the normal reaction of a dominant majority indignant that its traditional rights and privileges should be contested. It is reaction that is often peevish, and always more or less concerted, with a view to creating economic worries in Quebec. But we should emphasize the difference with the Americans who have seen many similar situations in other countries and who have not developed this menaced superiority complex so strongly felt by the Anglo-Canadians.

The Anglo-Canadians are more or less the traditional bosses, but they are more or less on the decline. The Americans are not particularly pleased by the possibility of turmoil north of the border, but neither are they disturbed to any great degree. We could therefore say that we do not anticipate any retaliation from the American quarter, providing that everything happens in an orderly fashion.

Given the fact that we know that Pepsi Cola is sold in countries in the Eastern bloc, and that Fiat is building factories there, etc., we can see for ourselves that beyond all these "Berlin walls" there is an economic interpenetration of regimes, even of those which are diametrically opposite to each other.

Rest assured! We are not another Cuba in the making, as some of our fiercest opponents would be pleased to have people believe. Nor are we a Chile. . . .

In all the immense agitation present in Quebec society, of what are you most aware?

The socio-economic problems of our time are not all necessarily directly related to the economy. They are also related to the giddy speed of the evolution of social relationships and the search for quality in life. New requirements are appearing on the horizon and I do not think that Quebec is any different from any other country in this respect. But in Quebec, more than elsewhere, the rapid democratization of teaching—access to secondary schools, followed by colleges and finally universities—has happened with extraordinary rapidity, because we have a lot of leeway to make up. This has increased incredibly the number of graduates, the number of those who consider themselves management potential, even though they do not always have the possibility of either employment or of advancement. This phenomenon creates serious complications and tensions within our society, especially as far as the participation of workers in all basic business decisions is concerned. For the working world, a change in society therefore consists of one part reorganization and another of mental readjustment on the part of the unions. There are tensions in business also. Employees, the young managers who are on the wave of the democratization which ran through education and which today is touching business, no longer accept the divine right, or what is left of it, of employers. And if we wish to avoid the pitfalls of improvisation and utopia of universal self management, we must begin to think about an adjustment towards a wider-based democracy in the internal structure of businesses.

By way of praise you often refer to the values of Quebecers as being those of a small surviving, different race. This disturbs the new immigrants, some of whom are beginning to talk about "Quebec racism."

One of the best tests of our position is to examine our attitude towards the Jews. There is a very large Jewish community in Quebec, which is centered principally in Montreal and which has been there for a long time. I think that the first Jews to arrive in Quebec travelled in the wagons of Wolfe's conquering army in the eighteenth century. The ancient regime in France was fairly hostile to Jews at that time. Perhaps it will surprise you to know that the first Jewish member of parliament elected in Canada was elected in Quebec, to the legislative assembly, as it was then called, by the region of Trois-Rivières. Now you cannot find a region more completely French than that! He was called Ezechiel Hart. He was opposed by the anglophone Quebecers of the period, and had to have his election reconfirmed by a second ballot. The second ballot merely reconfirmed the first decision of the electors and he was therefore well and truly re-elected. We should also note, à propos of the Jewish community, that their enormous business successes are based on the sale of everyday consumer items. This is the case with groceries: the Steinberg chain of stores belongs to citizens of the Jewish faith. Furthermore, everything concerned with massive consumerism in Quebec involves its 80 per cent of francophones. (It could be said that this is a sector of collective interest and yet, undeniably, it belongs for the most part to representatives of the Jewish community). On the other hand the sectors controlled by our anglophone friends, and over which they still have excessive control, are all the financial sectors. It is here that, if you scratch a little, you will find that polite, salon racism reigns. I really do not know why we are accused of racism because this has never been in French Quebec's line!

French Quebec is a society that is instinctively as open as any in the world. It conforms readily enough to the ancestral tradition of the coureurs des bois. Our history is one of opening up, especially towards the Indians. Today, if we rummage a little into the past, each one of us is proud to say, whenever he has the opportunity, that he has some Indian blood. The fact is that 40 per cent to 45 per cent of francophone Quebecers have Indian blood, which signifies that they were one of the white communities on the continent which best accepted mixing with others which is not at all common in the North American tradition. Our relatively harmonious co-existence with the Indians, the first owners of this land, has always existed, although there have certainly been moments of friction.

However, I also freely recognize that at certain times in our history we did exhibit feelings almost of dislike against newcomers. Remember that we have always been a minority community that remained rural for a long time, which always implies a lot of mistrust. Our society always retained its bitterness at having been conquered, and therefore at having been possessed by others. At certain moments of difficulty in our economy—I refer to the years of the Great Depression—some groups perhaps were resentful or negative towards others. I remember, for example, a slogan which was often used in those days—but I should also say that it was not unique to us—and which went: "Down with foreigners, they are after our jobs."

I have never thought it could be categorized as racism in the precise sense of the word to reject others because they are different. Wanting to slow down the arrival of foreigners for economic reasons is not racism. Whether they are white, black or yellow, Catholic, Protestant or Jewish, has nothing to do with the desire to save employment when it is threatened. This is doubtless perhaps an excessive reaction in relation to economic problems, but I repeat, denial of others because they are different has never been felt in Quebec. I can even cite a flagrant example: we are without a doubt the first province where a relatively recent immigrant has been elected as member of the National Assembly by a francophone constituency. This was the case with M. Jean Alfred, a Haitian teacher who married a Quebecer by birth. We also have some mayors and councilors in large municipalities, in francophone regions, who are colored.

All the polls indicate that the young generation believes in your option. What do you see in these young Quebecers?

First we must establish some distinction over and above the universal characteristics which define "youth" today. An adolescent is an adolescent everywhere. To a certain extent from certain points of view, he is the same at all latitudes, but over and above these universal characteristics we must distinguish within Quebec between anglophone youth and francophone youth. On the anglophone side most of them are still, like their parents, imbued with the Canadian dimension. They have fairly negative reactions towards any movement for the affirmation, the emancipation, and the collective promotion of French Quebec. But they represent only 15 to 20 per cent of the whole of Quebec youth.

As a general rule, the young participate in the Quebec nationalist movement and in the affirmation of the French people in Quebec. They are impatient for liberation. One sometimes has the impression that they are already living in a sovereign Quebec, which explains the difficulties we sometimes have in making them work on projects which are steps, but only steps, towards sovereignty. These young people say that they are French speaking, and that they are therefore in their own land. Their impatience, and their mistaken sentiment that they are already sovereign require us to move quickly. But on the other hand the fact that they are basking in the climate of the affirmation of French Quebec is one of the fundamental elements of our hope for the future. As a group they are coherent, and when the time comes to vote our soundings indicate that more than 75 per cent of them will choose our option. However this youth, anglophone and francophone together, is also a North American youth. As far as consumerism, tourism and education are concerned they are true products of American society. We are counting on this generation. Inevitably. Otherwise we would be counting more on the past than on the future. Whatever they are, with their faults and their qualities, they are already the present. This makes me very confident of the future, because the

North American mentality feeds on the possibilities of rapid advancement and accelerated maturity.

Precisely because they are already the present, do you not think that these young people will very soon play the role of the establishment?

However little one progresses in life, one always becomes part of an establishment somewhere! But it is true that it could happen here more swiftly than elsewhere. Unlike many European countries, where one has to scale every step of a career, in Quebec one can reach more quickly and more directly towards one's goals in a less planned, less linear fashion.

Already in the movement towards independence we can see the haste of some Quebecers to take the place of Anglo-Canadians or of those who favor federalism. Do you not fear an untimely witch hunt?

Let us understand each other. In any society in the process of self-affirmation, there is a thrust of elites who have multiplied over a period of fifteen or twenty years and whose potential as a result becomes more and more perceptible. These people are constantly beating against the wall constituted by the permanent occupation of many posts by minority, but dominant, interests. The whole history of emancipation rests on a certain thrust of elites.

Revolutions have always been started by the bourgeoisie. Why should Quebecers be any better than anyone else? That a certain elite is thinking about occupying a post which he thinks is due to him seems to me to be perfectly natural. At that level ambition, whether it is that of an individual or of a group, seems to me to be absolutely legitimate. It is not trying to do harm to others, in their country. It is saying simply: stop doing it to us, in ours!

Will a sovereign Quebec have all the skilled civil servants it will require?

As far as competent administrators are concerned, they have been available since the eighteenth century, before confederation, and since then with our status as a semi-state or as a province. We have more than a hundred years of tradition in many sectors such as education, legislation and public administration, as well as in the sectors which have taken on increasing importance in our time such as everything connected with social security (although many controls currently rest under federal tutelage). The same applies to the management of the land. However, there we are running into all sorts of encroachments and overlaps from the federal government and we still have no control over anything to do with sea ports, airports, the railway, nor with their employees, because they are in the federal domain. This all contrives to maintain an absolutely irrational and often absurd distortion in the distribution and the management of the infrastructures of our territory. But as far as the balance to be established between urbanization, the protection of rural zones, urban planning or densification is concerned, much experience has been accumulated, and we are ready. I should add that we were enormously backward in some domains. We have had to make enormous efforts in finding ways of correcting this. The job will never be perfect but our efforts at education and self promotion, according to UNESCO estimates, are the most efficient and the most spectacular of any western society.

In 1968-69 we had 52,000 enrolments in our universities. By 1975-76 this number had almost doubled to 96,000—with, we know, all the dangers which this intensive increase can bring, but also with all the valuable benefits of such a development in the level of education. More and more educated people are emerging who, little by little, are framing our society as well as, and certainly no worse than, others have been doing in our place. A certain number of institutions are evolving whose excellence is beginning to be recognized outside. For example, we possess certainly one of the best business administration schools in North America, the *École des hautes études commerciales*, whose reputation is known all over the continent. Our *École polytechnique* is also counted among the best. The only really backward area, which we are trying to improve, is in research centers. However, these deficiencies do not prevent us from being certain that we can fulfill our needs for administrators and for skills. It is absolutely necessary for us to get rid of the last trappings of the inferiority complex which derives from our over-lengthy colonial history and, in the economic and administrative domain, from too long a period during which we were systematically deprived of a hold on the control mechanisms. Here is an example.

When we created the *Caisse de dépôts et placements* (in 1965-66 under the Lesage government of which I was a member), a list of candidates for the presidency of this body, which was going to become, very quickly, an investor of several billions of dollars, was submitted to us. Among the suggested ·candidates was one of the vice presidents of a large insurance company called Sun Life. He was a francophone Quebecer. He knew the subject. And he set up the business remarkably well. When this suggestion for the candidacy was put before the cabinet, I remember that we asked ourselves in anguish who this obscure vice president was, and whether he really had the capability of going further in Sun Life, the company which employed him, and was he simply stuck at this level because he was a francophone? These were the questions generated in our group. We had to cut through this incertitude. The sequel showed us that we were right to have confidence in him. The way in which the *Caisse de dépôts* developed, with no grave errors during its formative period, shows that he was certainly competent enough to be the president of Sun Life and of other companies at the same time, because today the *Caisse de dépôts* could easily digest a few of them!

Do you see the possibility of an exodus on the part of the new educated elites in Quebec?

No, as far as francophone graduates of the universities are concerned we do not foresee anything of this kind, but this phenomenon does exist in the anglophone universities which are subsidized, like others, to the extent of 80 per cent out of public funds. At McGill University which is in a state of relative decline, 50 per cent or more of the students in some expensive faculties such as medicine, come from English Canada, the United States or abroad. We talk about it sometimes, with irony. McGill has become a rather grand university within the anglophone commonwealth but it depends on Quebec for 80 per cent of its funding. There is no question of our becoming a ghetto, or of closing our doors to foreigners. But to supply, from here, doctors and dentists for our American friends who are richer than we are, that certainly cannot last forever.

Who is your model politician?

I do not believe in a model politician any more than I believe in a model society. When one is active in government one must look for sustenance everywhere and not imagine that one can find absolute models.

I have, however, always had a preference for Roosevelt who to my mind was a very great president of the United States. Napoleon also I found fascinating when I was a young student, but that is an age when one often dreams of being a conqueror! When I found out about all the crimes and plundering committed during the Consulate and the Empire, I developed a rather cooler attitude towards him.

Roosevelt, as leader of the American people, and occasionally as a fairly cynical practitioner of politics, is one of the most extraordinary figures in the twentieth century. I can also add without the least hesitation a more recent example, Charles de Gaulle, for his high aspirations and for his grandiose excesses especially during the war when he claimed alone, to be the embodiment of a whole people.

And now, since I have been in power and have lost a certain number of my illusions, I feel myself closest perhaps to J.F. Kennedy (or to the socialist theoretician Antonio Gramsci), because the most difficult thing for a politician is to retain one's ideals even as one loses all one's illusions.

What is your model economic organization?

In 1972 the Parti Québécois published a manifesto entitled: *Quand nous serons vraiment chez nous.* This manifesto, which has retained all its topicality, gives a lot of space to economic questions and to their social impact. It is the most valid justification for the political sovereignty that we are claiming. It is also the justification for the hypothesis of association with Canada. It arrives at three conclusions. First, this economy is dated in many vital sectors. Second, this economy is badly balanced. It is only partly absorbing the great waves of industrialization of the twentieth century. Iron and steel and mechanical construction developed late, and only partially. It is also an economy which is too foreign to Quebec society. We have too few local entrepreneurs. The decision-making centers are located outside our society in the Anglo-Canadian caste in Montreal, and currently American interests in Canada are managed by administrators from this same, anglophone group. A mentality of dependence has developed. The provincial governments, our "negro kings," have often refused to take any initiative which might harm, even in the tiniest degree, foreign interests. And the federal government has accentuated this sentiment of powerlessness by increasing the number of social subsidies instead of developing a responsible economy as has been the case in Ontario and in the West.

We refuse to follow the "maximalists" who would like to move along a revolutionary path. Contrary to what they say, sovereignty is not a "petit bourgeois" objective, modernization of the government does not foretell a form of state capitalism. Objectively, if we were to move in their direction we would break up into cliques, condemned to powerlessness and the perennity of the *status quo*. We must never forget that Quebec needs to learn, like most modern peoples, that rationality and strength in government are still the source of development. Vigor does not exclude lucidity. Between the revolution for new soviets and the "gradualism" of those who, deep down, want to change nothing of importance, there is room for radicalism doubled with realism. Quebec has enough savings and enough competent people to be able to reduce unemployment, increase the standard of living and practice regional development.

Could you define "social democracy" as you understand it?

It has not been emphasized enough that it has taken a hundred years for "social democracy" to reach the state of the "Swedish model", which is now being contested since there have been elections recently and Mr. Olaf Palme has been replaced. The English version of social democracy which took over in 1945 when Churchill was overthrown in the aftermath of the war is something different, which is different again from the German socio-economic regime.

It is useless to try and make social democracy comparable everywhere at a certain point in the evolution of a country, for the fact is that the histories of Sweden, of England, and of Federal Germany have nothing in common with our own. Our social democracy will be a Quebec social democracy, or it will not be.

We have to translate into concrete projects that which we consider to be most important, which is to say first and foremost, equality of opportunity for everyone. This implies many readjustments which cannot be made from one day to the next.

Another element in our model is the distribution of incomes. We do not yet, as a province, have the power to reduce to any great extent disparities in incomes. Furthermore, I do not think that total equality is possible in this domain because we would then have a society which would no longer have any incentive. Even the most dogmatic socialist regimes have differences between salaries in order to generate motivation. Canada and Quebec are not among those countries where the differences are the greatest, but there is nonetheless a lot to do in this specific domain. The third element is one which I hold very dear to my heart: this is the participation of the citizen, a participation which we hope will be as great as possible and which will leave hollow words and phrases behind and enter fully into the reality of people's lives. This implies for us, as it would everywhere else but especially for us because of the dimensions of our territory, a real decentralization.

It will not be enough to "deconcentrate" administration, as the traditional jargon goes, by installing local civil servants. We have to arrive at an effective decentralization by allocating true responsibility, and accompanying it with budgetary resources. At the local and at the regional level, citizens must be able to check those who are responsible for budgets and services as closely as possible. This is one of the grand plans, and certainly one of the most delicate, which we are trying to pursue today. Our territory and the dispersion of our population give a note of urgency to this preoccupation—responsibility of the individual citizen—which is essential in our eyes. The citizen must be able to intervene in his own affairs, which implies in consequence the right of workers to participate in decisions concerning their business life and their working conditions. Experiments of this kind have already been tried in certain countries, especially in Scandinavia.

The Swedish kind of capitalism seems to hold an unquestionable attraction for you. . . .

The Swedish experience undoubtedly holds a certain attraction for us because they are a northern people and so their situation is relatively comparable to ours from the point of view of population, climate and basic resources. But we should not push this relatively simplistic connection too far. Sweden has had fifty years' experience in the formation of its socio-democratic model, to which it has just, perhaps temporarily, applied the brakes.

Though it should not deprive itself of useful inspiration, including that of Sweden, Quebec must find its own path. On a continent which is still the capitalist Mecca of the world, and which has found the means to bend its capitalism more quickly and further than any other place (I do not want to say that it is paradise) where and how do we stand? This is where "gradualism" comes into the picture. Our principal exports are to the North American market, an essential part of our imports originate from American production lines, and the markets for capital from which we cannot sever ourselves are in New York, Chicago, and increasingly in Europe. But this network of interrelations is in a constant state of flux, and we must maintain some of the continental links which are essential to us. We cannot, whatever happens, break with the American context and American thinking. Our plan will lead to something completely different from what we over-simply call "neo capitalism." Through what stages? Through what changes? We will see. I have great confidence in the evolutionary capacity of a country such as Quebec. During the period of evolution towards our own model which we will baptize later, the "social democratic" label which has been affixed to us suits us well providing we can write our own definition of the phrase.

You are not Castro, and Quebec is no Cuba, but do you not fear that some people might boycott this new Quebec?

In economics, social democracy is a kind of step by step rhythm in one's demands along with acceptance of living with others. In North America we know very well what that means.

Foreign interests, though they participate in the development of Quebec, do not come here out of love and to help us to survive but because it is profitable for them to do so, because they reap dividends. This applies today. It will apply tomorrow. Because there are measures for which it is impossible to find substitutes. This is the case with asbestos where we have remained extraordinarily important exporters. It is the case with the pulp and paper necessary to feed the enormous appetites of the *New York Times* and the *Chicago Tribune*, which is treated directly in mills which are vertically integrated with the newspaper empires, in a captive market. Here again I can see no substitution in the immediate future. The same applies to iron ore which remains one of the most accessible, the most certain, and practically inexhaustible of Quebec's resources even though technological progress in the fifties made iron ore extensively available through the world.

Investors never knock profitability as long as political conditions allow them, even though it might be with great difficulty, to exploit their business.

Although we are not satisfied with the balance of our economic development, Quebec, with its six million inhabitants, is among those with the highest standards of living in the world. The market in a city such as Montreal represents such an intensive area of consumerism that it must necessarily be served, and those who take the risks of boycotting it will be replaced with no difficulty. Any investor knows this.

At what speed could you evolve towards this new regime?

Democracy, as I see it, should respect the capacity for evolution of a society. Certainly we must not use this argument as a mask for timorous prudence, for delaying decisions and changes which must be made, but we must to a certain degree "sound" a society in order for it to arrive, step by step, at its objectives. All this must be accompanied by constant respect, which demands that we remain close to society, that we live within the society, and that power does not cut us off from the man in the street.

We will try never to forget that we must respect the capacity for absorption of reforms and change, and respect the rules and regulations of democracy.

How has Quebec managed to safeguard its independence of its neighbor, the United States?

For us, colonization began with a military conquest at the end of the Seven Years War in the eighteenth century, which was followed very shortly by the American War of Independence. England was in conflict both with a new colony, numerically insignificant, of 60,000 to 70,000 French colonists and with its special colony, its other self, ie., the states of New England, the thirteen future independent states. As events unfolded, England panicked to an increasing degree and decided that it had to set up a rearguard action. All this happened in less than fifteen years, from 1760-63 to 1774-75. In 1774 England was driven to grant rights which might seem a little extravagant for a newly conquered people. These rights were granted in 1774 in the Quebec Act. England conceded the right to use French in Quebec, the use of the French civil code, and a whole series of concessions designed to recognize various fundamental rights, including those in the domain of religion. The Quebec Act would have been completely out of the question if it had not been for some special circumstances. England was on the eve of war with the New England states. This was therefore a form of insurance for them at the time. The agreements corresponded completely to our society under the ancient regime, which still had a very deeply imbued suspicion of words such as "democracy" and "republic" which were being heard from its American neighbors.

With the Quebec Act, therefore, which guaranteed our society many fundamental rights, our colonization started under extremely favorable auspices, and for a very long time the English regime wore the image of a protector. As one might have expected, this did not prevent the usual takeover of our society by conquering interests, especially in the economic domain. One concrete example is the fur trade which, along with that of two or three other very basic products, including timber, was in the hands of the francophones, and trade was conducted with the French-speaking world. After the conquest the fur trade was immediately monopolized by the agents of the conquering army—as always happens. This was the case with one character called McGill, an ingenious man, a Scotsman, who are eternal entrepreneurs and are often the most brilliant bankers. This Scotsman, McGill, having become the fur king, created a foundation with his personal fortune, and in the 1820's opened an English university in Montreal, while the first, very poor and very humble university, a descendent of the old Quebec seminary, emerged in Quebec under the name of Laval University only in the middle of the nineteenth century. This is a perfect illustration of foreign colonization. On the other hand, some resentment towards French Quebec was born in the anglophone society, and this was certainly linked to notions of the British Empire, and also to the fact that they had not completely forgotten their old bitterness towards Napoleon and even the Seven Years War. The feeling was reciprocated on the French side. The two solitudes interpenetrated only with difficulty.

The steamroller of the United States has already integrated many countries into its system. Do you have all the cards you need for your policy of independence? Is there not a risk that your evolution towards sovereignty will fail?

There are always risks. History is strewn with risks. But the general climate of a wakening or reawakening of conscience does not exist solely in Quebec. Think of the Scots, or what is happening to the Walloons, or to the Slovaks facing the Czechs.

On a world scale I am a federalist. Why? It is very simple. If we do not one day succeed in eliminating two of the horsemen of the Apocalypse, war and hunger, I think that there will be tragedy in the world. Such possibilities of chaos could be avoided if we were to adopt the elements of a mini-federalism. International society must succeed in declawing the mighty and the beasts of prey, in order to allow the rest to breathe. It seems to me that this potential trend should be encouraged. The need for it is obvious on a world scale.

Alongside the phenomenon of decolonization, however, we can see a rebirth occurring in all culturally distinct societies, or at least in those which have the slightest chance of giving themselves a political armor, those which have their language, their identity, their traditions, their own land,—a piece of ground where they can sink their roots and the hope of a better future. This awakening is almost universal, wherever there exists a chance, however small it might be, to identify oneself a little more precisely than previously. Every people would like, as far as possible, to distinguish itself from others because, in the face of the more or less homogenizing current running through the world, which is accentuated by technical and economic factors, every identity feels a need to affirm its presence in order to avoid disappearing. One could very well adopt a minimal degree of federalism on a world scale, while remaining extremely nationalistic—nationalist in the sense of national sovereignty, and the affirmation of one's identity.

You are trying to conduct a dialogue with the people. Is this effort not imposed because your government is essentially made up of technicians, intellectuals and members of the liberal professions?

There are certainly more intellectuals than in the governments that preceded us. This is also true for the Parti Québécois as all the surveys and internal reports have proved. The Parti Québécois has recruited a large number, almost a disproportionate number of people, who have received certificates in higher education, but this has not prevented our base from growing larger each year for the last six years. The 1976 elections proved this: the P.Q. won more than 41 per cent of the total vote and therefore a majority of the French vote, since the 20 per cent of anglophones do not particularly favor our program. It is therefore evident that the party is beginning to establish roots in many milieus. It is neither an ivory tower nor a chapel of the intelligentsia. The presence of "intellectuals" is evident, however, in a good proportion of the current deputation in the Assembly. But if you were to compare with the preceding generations, you would notice in equally large numbers either the old or the new rich, lawyers, doctors, professors, or administrators. It is perhaps a little more marked in our case, but we have not reached the point where they should be considered as a foreign body.

Will you yourselves not, over the course of time, and as a result of various pressures, come to appear as a sort of establishment and cut yourselves off from your party?

This is always a risk which a reasonably democratic government finds it difficult to avoid. One always ends up, one fine day, by being a little too establishment and thereby cutting oneself off from reality. I think it was Napoleon who said: "The facts are stubborn" and if one day we pass them by without seeing them, because power has a fatal tendency to try and mask certain areas of neglect and certain omissions, we will pay the price. This is why governments change. In order to delay such an eventuality we must remain open and practice a policy of presence. The citizens are our employers. We must, with tours and impromptu visits, retain a constant physical presence. I have requested of the members of Parliament, and therefore all the ministers, that we should each stay in our constituencies at least twice a year and systematically, for a certain number of days during the sessional breaks. In addition, I have asked that the ministers, this time as representatives of the government, participate in tours which will not be partisan, and will not have anything to do with propaganda, but which will be well and truly for the purpose of reporting progress. These should take place approximately every six months. People are to be given explanations of what we are doing, what we are planning. In return we get questions about things where people are not in agreement with us, along with ideas and complaints. In summary, I believe in a constant dialogue with the population.

How are relations between the P. Q., which like every party may take some extreme positions, and the government, which like any executive must take into account realities?

It is always difficult to maintain a balance in the relationship between the militant party and the government, i.e., between members of Parliament, the Cabinet and those responsible for the administration. This balance is even harder to achieve if we are dealing with a party . . . of the left or let us say of the center left in any case. . . .

Our party believes in democratic discussion, internal democracy, contestation and even dissidence when it appears to be required. All this is very sound. It is inevitable that there wll be tensions between the party and the executive. For my part I feel that this tension is fruitful, and I believe that it is present in all the social democratic or socialist parties in power as long as they remain open to the democratic spirit. A government should not bow to the party, because it must be the government of all the citizens, but it must nonetheless consider the party as a moral political leader and respect whatever morality it represents.

We must follow—but never blindly—the directions the party has established or is continuing to establish for itself. We certainly felt this tension at the congress we held in May 1977 where it was necessary on certain points for me to say, in the name of the government, that it was not possible to accept some resolutions which emanated from the assembly. The P.Q. accepted this, but the situation created some stress, which in itself is not a bad thing at all. Conversely, I would consider it fatal if the party were now to fall asleep, telling itself that it was in power and could therefore let the government take care of everything.

By making a distinction in your Cabinet between ministers and superministers, have you not threatened the cohesion of the Cabinet?

In November 1976, we recreated, or redefined, the notion of the Minister of State. We did not go as far as an inner and an outer Cabinet as they have in England, but we had to at least reduce the risk of incoherence in a group of twenty-five—and sometimes more—ministers, who are constantly trying to sort out priorities, break down barriers and co-ordinate their activities.

The five ministers of state, along with the large horizontal sectors under the ministers of finance, and intergovernmental affairs make up the priorities committee. The ministers of state reach this committee armed with the work of the permanent sectorial committee for which they are responsible. For example, there are permanent committees on cultural, social, and economic development. The ministers of state are responsible for guiding these committees, co-ordinating their activities, and participating, with the premier and the horizontal ministers, in the work of adjusting priorities. They acquaint their colleagues in the Cabinet with their points of view. They are not superministers. They perhaps appear to have a slightly predominant role because they co-ordinate and because they participate in this preselecting of priorities, but all matters are brought up again before a full meeting of the Cabinet and decisions are taken by the group as a whole. It is only the roles that are different. The role of co-ordinating, of piloting to a certain extent, is one which I think that no government today can do without. If this experiment had failed we would have had to try something else, because any government which prepares and co-ordinates its action, in however small a way, must have something along the lines of this method of division of tasks.

It is whispered that your Cabinet is not the most homogeneous and people are looking for signs of dissension or even a split among Cabinet members. Are many non-unanimous decisions made?

In our party there are people who have extremely precise convictions and motivations on one or another aspect of social, or economic or cultural questions. This does not always make it easy for us to reach any degree of unanimity, but the tradition of the Cabinet being to avoid a vote, it is eventually necessary either to produce a concensus or else to let a matter ride. If an emergency occurs we must, whatever the price, arrive at a point where everyone accepts that a position of solidarity has been achieved, even if it takes two or three days or two or three nights to reach this point. The Cabinet has functioned on this basis since November 1976. This does not mean that there have been no instances of reservation and that some people have not been obliged to "swallow" some decisions. This is natural. However, I always act in the perspective of the consensus which must necessarily evolve at the end.

Ottawa's centralism is subtle. They dispel suspicion by adroitly arguing common interest. Do you think that Quebecers have as acute an awareness as you do of what appears to you to be a trap?

I think that the Quebecers are becoming more and more aware of the dangers of this trap because it has been going on for thirty years and increasing constantly. This federal trespassing is generally sly, sometimes blatant. It has facades, like the one they called "French power," which can fool people for a certain period of time but which will not prevent the camouflage from suddenly disapproving eventually. When the question of economic responsibilities arises, for example, the majority of Quebecers are beginning very seriously to put the responsibility where it lies, which is with the federal regime and the administration. They know full well that the principal levers are manouvered from there and that the principal gaffes are also committed there. Furthermore, their natural sympathies, and the surveys prove this, are towards the government of Quebec as it stands at this time . . . even though many people hope to transform it. This government, with its faults and its qualities, derives from our society. From its potential also. It is the only one over which we have the total grasp which a society should have over its institutions.

Canada already has a certain amount of difficulty in maintaining its economic autonomy in relation to the American economy. Will American and international finance not discriminate against Quebec?

On the map Canada appears to be enormous but it is in fact a country of only twenty-three people disseminated along the border of the United States. The security, the stability and the possibility of self development, the achievement of a certain amount of economic emancipation by this population of twenty-three million stretched out like a long worm along a frontier, are no more difficult than for six million people who, with their own language, their common history and a well placed territory, would form a compact people within the framework of their own institutions. In fact, I would give the greater chance to this sufficiently compact and well-integrated people, rather than to the soft body constituted by the Canadian entity. This is not flippant, it is a deduction which anyone in Canada might make. When our detractors announce fatalistically the unavoidable satellization of Quebec by the United States, I really have to ask myself if the American entity could go further than the point to which Canada has descended. If Canada has at this point become a satellite of the American economic empire, then this has happened as a result of basic decisions taken by the Anglo-Canadian majority and by the federal government by virtue of political and economic powers vested in the federal government and imposed on all the provinces, including Quebec. Whatever happens, a sovereign Quebec will be less stifled, less powerless, than it is at present.

Ottawa has found nothing better than the creation of a filtering agency in answer to a fairly diffused pan-Canadian sense of nationalism. This very discretionary, and also very discreet, agency which monitors foreign investments, is one whose activities are extremely difficult to follow clearly, and it has so far changed absolutely nothing of any importance. Over and above those activities which a provincial state could develop and which were laid down in the sixties we had already chosen, before we were in government and in preparation for the time when we would be in power, with our code of investments, an option for economic self government, without which political sovereignty risks becoming nothing more than a hollow shell.

Instead of intervening step by step, factory by factory, as the federal agency did, we will treat the economy by sectors and we will take those measures necessary for a self respecting national economy which accepts the fact that it will have to change gradually. We will proceed in stages, disturbing nothing, in such a way as to avoid losses in profitability and adverse political repercussions. We will progressively emancipate that which needs to be emancipated in order to ensure that we are masters of all essential decisions in an increasingly interdependent world. We will be the ones to decide whether a business will be private, public, or mixed. But as often as possible ownership will be in Quebec.

What is your position towards the United States?

I have spent a whole portion of my life, as have many journalists, in constant contact with North America and especially with the closest states, New England, New York States, and Chicago. However, I have never been one of those who has borne against the United States that simplistic anti-Americanism, which is almost inevitable, that the reality of this enormous empire sometimes unleashes. We have to admit that we are living in the era of the American culture. This is a culture with a universal dimension, which is omnipresent. The world basks in the influence of, and subscribes to American values. As Quebecers we are even closer to it, and to be unaware of its influence and to founder in anti-American feeling seems to me to be completely puerile. Furthermore, the American intellectual tradition, far from being negligeable, is much greater than some fine minds imagine it to be. The United States has all the faults of a great power, except organized ghettos, concentration camps and bloodbaths. Despite Vietnam and certain CIA activities, it remains the most liveable of all empires hitherto known, and one which has the possibility of becoming even more civilized, or at any rate much more so than many other powers.

I have retained enormous admiration for many of their achievements. I will start with the founding fathers of the United States. It suffices to read what they had to say, to immerse oneself in the atmosphere of the times, to understand that it was as extraordinary an event in the history of the world as the miracle of Athens in ancient Greece. I have always found this combination of genius and absolutely extraordinary perspective in a small colony of three or four million very inspiring. Of all the achievements of the American society, I always recall particular aspects, such as their fundamental egalitarianism. Every American can say to himself: "The president and me, it's the same thing. We are Americans, we are citizens of America just like him."

And more openness in relationships, which to some extent is something we share. There is also a very practical and tenacious side to the Americans which I would quite often like to see increasingly evident here: "We must produce, we must make it happen." American fiber is pragmatic fiber and it marks every aspect of society. The great American sociologists, who very often study questions which are of enormous interest to us, are clinical sociologists. They go directly to the point of reality. Our humanist molding, on the other hand, often leads us from theories first to generalizations and subsequently, later, to see whether the reality could bend itself to the generalizations. There are many lessons to be learned from American pragmatism.

Among your colleagues there are many who favor a European contribution.

And this makes an excellent balance! I cannot underestimate the European contribution, primarily because it was the source of our living culture. Everything in our culture, our language, all we have inherited by way of technical matter, science, even of administration, is of European origin. But our membership in the American world should allow us to invigorate and strengthen the ancient cultural ties which link us with Europe. The dividing line between European culture and American culture does not pass between one person and another; it is something that is within each one of us.

What place do you want to establish for Quebec on the international scene?

We must retain a very modest perspective in international politics because, and experience throughout the world proves this, international policies develop as a function of circumstances. There are some essential parameters which are dictated by the geography of each country and by its permanent interests. Certainly adjustments are made, but to claim to be able to foresee them and to be able to chart them in advance seems to me not only presumptious, but ridiculous.

Especially since we do not have the experience, nor do we have our hand on the necessary controls, as long as we are still only a province. Certain relationshps, which remain closely watched over by Ottawa, have been established as a result of the network of eighteen Quebec delegations, and our flock of young "coopérants" around the world. These are the beginnings of international relations which would give us some initial experience.

As a party and as a government, the only thing we have in our program in anticipation of the day it will be required is a thorough definition of our basic attitudes, in the light of our geographic situation and our permanent interests such as they appear to us today.

The fundamentals are very simple: first, we must classify in a hierarchical order of priority the relations we need to establish. Relationships to be permanently adjusted as fast as possible, with Canada first of all, for the obvious reason of our association, with the United States for no less obvious reasons, and finally with Europe and the francophone countries, of which the foremost is obviously France. The fundamental triangle of our foreign relations will be Canada, the United States and Europe, beginning with France and the French speaking countries. As far as the rest is concerned, we will have to follow broad principles. For example, in our opinion the small countries have a role to play as active promoters of peace. The example of the Scandinavian countries in this respect would be an excellent one to follow because they often play the role of agents of reconciliation and peacemakers between different peoples.

What do you think of the Western left wing parties, and of Eurocommunism?

What interested me the most on the subject of the European left wing was the recent debate on southern socialism and northern socialism. What emerged from that was the image of a much more dogmatic and much more hard line socialism in the south of the continent, in France, Italy, Spain and Portugal. On the other hand the socialism of the north seemed more evolutionary, more empirical. I confess that of the two points of view I was more akin to that of the north.

As far as evolution is concerned, one thing strikes me first of all: the Common Market is in the process of changing many situations. There are also many changes arising out of the democratization of Spain and Portugal since the last elections, and also out of the historical compromise accepted by the communist party in Italy. I cannot make any judgment about what happens in these groups because I do not know them. But Italian communism seems to want to adjust to a particular evolution of society which would enable it to play the democratic game and to participate in government. This would bring it close to the attempted Union of the Left in France, which is probably the only way for these groups to take power providing they do not divide, or fall again into conflict within their own ranks.

Your province wants to withdraw from a federal system, while the European states are on the point of electing a parliament.

If a European Parliament is formed, and if it is given real powers, it will be this body that governs, and at that moment they will understand why we Quebecers do not like organic federalism in its ancient mode. In Europe, for continental reasons, it is in certain minds that they should create a super power which should be able to stand on its own in planetary dialogue with the East as much as with the American empire, with the Japanese power which is emerging more and more, and eventually with China. This dream of European grandeur would seem to demand that this power should be politically honed to a very fine degree. From this point of view I can completely understand the idea of the European Parliament, but will this not merely be falling back into a multinational, multicultural federalism? Will it not be a retrograde step into the formulae of the eighteenth or nineteeth century which was really applicable only where there was a cultural melting pot, which is not the case with Europe? The United States, with all its problems, is nonetheless one of the most effective melting pots. The same applies to Federal Germany which, with all its provincial nuances, is totally German speaking.

Binational federations such as the Canadian federation, or multinational federation, are to my mind paths which turn into cul-de-sacs. But that is the Europeans' affair.

We have believed for many years, and we will continue to believe, in the brilliant imagination which conceived the new formula of the Treaty of Rome. To borrow from General de Gaulle's expression, "A Europe of homelands" was and remains one of the roads open for the future in a world where each cultural or national entity wishes to express itself as never before, but where at the same time there is another current moving in the sense of unification. As a means of balancing the two it seems to me that the formula of the Common Market, the formula of the Nine, or eventually of the Twelve, permits on the one hand a continuation of affirmation of identity and on the other hand a response to the need to enlarge markets, to have increasingly intense communication between people. I think that by now throwing themselves into a federal structure and electing a parliament they are breaking the natural course of development of the Common Market.

My reaction is no doubt typically North American, or at any rate that of a man raised in the British tradition, which is to think thus: with or without a parliament, whether on the scale of individual countries or on the scale of this parliament, what is most necessary is to leave behind the tradition of the "old" Europe, with its narrow and very often doctrinaire compartments, and replace the "salad" composed of all the small parties which are never in the majority, and construct in their place two or three large parties which would represent the principal currents in society and would also simplify these currents.

Are you counting on the support of the European social-democrats?

Absolutely not. We will have contact with them certainly. On a personal level, some members of our government, since they have visited them, already know the Scandinavian countries and northern Europe, in addition to Germany. We are not counting on the correspondence between our societies and our economies to take the decision that has to be taken in Quebec. If, at the time of the referendum, Quebec makes its decision in the direction we propose, it is probable during the period of transition and in the early stages which follow that there will be a degree of empathy shown by these social democratic regimes.

We are counting to a greater degree on the natural correspondence which should be established between us and those cultural milieus which are closely related to ours, which is to say the French and the Walloons, even though Quebec is not always as well known there as we could wish. Quebec has not often been violently spoken of in the course of history! But we have nonetheless many enlightened friends, in France notably, among the Walloons, and in the Swiss Jura, and we hope that this natural relationship between us will come into play when the time comes. There is much comfort for us in knowing that we can communicate with friends, with people who understand our problems, and who see the future, even if it is not their own future, in the same manner as we do, because after all we are all jointly and severally responsible in the world. But we are not expecting anything further by way of support.

The amount of the loans raised by Quebec on the German market is very large. Do you have the impression that you are well received there?

Yes, Quebec's credit is pretty good throughout the world. Like Switzerland or any other financial establishment, Germany evaluates the economic strength and the nature of the guarantees afforded by its borrowers very coldly. This is the only thing that counts. For the most part, financial circles are absolutely unconcerned about political ideology. They generally favor the *status quo*.

The German market has been tapped on occasion, in a relatively modest fashion, in our European operations, which do not by a long way compare with the size of our natural market in Quebec, Canada and the United States. Our internal market is already very large. Even though Quebec has only six million inhabitants it is, per capita, one of the largest reservoirs of capital in the world. The tradition of saving runs very strong in Quebec. The accumulation of capital represents between thirty and thirty-five billion dollars. We are also retaining our opening into the Canadian market. As long as we are politically linked with Canada, we are so financially also, which does not mean that Toronto is doing us any favors. They do not much like Quebec's political orientation there, but Anglo-Canadians could soon find themselves in a vicious circle. If they try to systematically boycott Quebec, they could accelerate its development in just the direction they do not want it to take. If, on the other hand, they respect the rules of the game, as we have undertaken to do until the people of Quebec make their decision, there is no reason for any boycotting. The operations of the government are essentially financed from inside. Hydro-Quebec, which needs a phenomenal amount of capital for its developments has had to call on outside markets for its own credit and with the state as guarantor.

But has the sum of the loans raised in the European markets not risen since the P.Q. came into power?

This is not new. For several years the European financial market has been dealing with Quebec loans. We want, progressively, to diversify our sources which have been isolated for too long in the United States, in New York and more rarely in Chicago. We have also taken into account the fact that the major expansion of the Europe of the Nine offers, from many points of view, a market equally important as that of the United States.

Like most of the provincial governments in Canada, which do not have a central bank and are not complete, established masters of their financial operations, Quebec must go to the market, like a business enterprise. With the reservation, however, that it is difficult for a government to become insolvent. The Bourassa government had already begun looking towards the European financial markets, but we intensified this practice during the first months of our administration, both to maintain the image of the financial soundness of Quebec and also to respond to our needs. However, we borrowed within a relatively austere framework. There will be no more simplistic politics, with cascades of loans, like those we allowed ourselves between 1974 and 1976.

BY WAY OF CONCLUSION (UNFINISHED)

"We are Quebecers"

. . . We are speaking of a people that for a long time has been content, to let itself be forgotten in order to survive. But then it said that in order to survive validly, one must assert one's identity, and subsequently that, in order to properly assert one's identity, it must become desirable and even necessary to be emancipated. A few days less than a year ago, therefore, a party acceded to power whose initial raison d'être was exactly this political emancipation, and despite what was claimed, and still is claimed by certain people who have not understood the significance of this event, the electors were neither heedless nor ignorant. They knew very well what they were doing. And many people, even some who were opposed to us, felt an enormous surge of pride in a victory over the kind of blackmail practiced by all those regimes which feel themselves threatened.

It is therefore more and more assured that a new country will soon appear, by democratic means, on the map, where until now a federal state would have preferred to see only one of its many provinces, and where those whom you often call *"les Français du Canada,"* an apparently simple expression, which rejoins the essential facts, but whose meaning has nonetheless become ambiguous over the course of time, have their home.

Let us begin with the indisputable facts it encompasses. Quebec measures approximately 2,000 kilometers from north to south, and more than 1,500 from east to west, and is therefore, physically, the largest country in the world whose official language is French. More than four out of five of its inhabitants are of French origin and culture. Outside Europe we are therefore the only large community which is of French stock. We can, like you, seriously evoke our ancestors, the Gauls! And as we are only six million in the corner of a continent which numbers forty times as many anglophones, we sometimes even feel encircled, like Asterix in his village. ... And imagine that the entire continent of North America ought to have been French instead of ... neo-Roman.

For indeed our beginnings were incredible. From Hudson's Bay and Labrador in the north to the Gulf of Mexico in the south, from the Gaspé near the Atlantic to the Rockies, from which one can almost see the Pacific, there we were—and there you were—as the discoverers and the first European settlers. When Champlain built his home in Quebec and Nouvelle France was born, the Mayflower pilgrims had not even raised anchor on their journey to found New England.

And so, for a hundred and fifty years soldiers and missionaries and colonists and coureurs des bois wrote a good number of the most extraordinary, if not the most famous, pages of the history of the seventeenth and eighteenth centuries.

When I was a little boy, like all children I had my own personal hero, whom I am sure I shared with many young Quebecers. His name was Pierre Lemoyne d'Iberville. Of all those who, through polar cold and torrid heat, forged a path across the New World, he was without doubt the most striking. If his theater of operation had not been these distant places or, if you will forgive my saying so, if France had been a little less exclusively rivetted to Europe, you would today have a multitude of little French boys who would also dream of being d'Iberville.

However, this history, for a century and a half, was ours—and also yours. And I remember that when we arrived at the last chapter, the one which ended with defeat and conquest, we lost the desire to know what followed, and instead returned indefatigably to the beginning; because what followed, with due respect to our British compatriots, seemed in some way to have become the history of another people.

And this defeat meant absolutely that, according to the true derivation of the word, which is to say that something as a result became undone, demolished, and for a long time. And this something was our "aptitude to become a normal nation," that an attendant to the king, like many other observers, had noted in one of his reports to Versailles. If French colonization, the weaker, had not had to fight against English colonization, which was the stronger, the evolution of the Canadians, a name which as yet no one used, would have led them to a full existence as a nation, just as surely, and not much later than the other thirteen colonies which later called themselves the United States.

This is not a nostalgic idealization of a tiny society of some tens of thousands of poor people who, in 1760 in the Saint Lawrence Valley, had to submit to a foreign domination which was destined to remain for a long time. As with all the other colonies of the time, this was as yet nothing more than a modest outgrowth of a metropolis which was both natural and distant, and whose power, once its job was done, should have ended with us as it did elsewhere had its continuity not been broken. Already in fact, distance, the climate, contact with the Indian population, the continental experience had fashioned a mentality and a way of life which were becoming more and more different from that of the mother country. This was a nation, and a French nation certainly, but a nation which was just as able to live its own life and to be a presence in the world as any other.

This is what defeat broke up, but it did not manage to dispel the dream. It was a dream which, though normally unacknowledged, was strong enough to nourish, even today, a national identity and a national idea that only numerical weakness and total isolation prevented us from realizing.

But soon the numbers began to increase and the "revenge from the cradle" multiplied them so prodigiously that the great historian Toynbee affirmed one day that, in his opinion, when the trumpets of the last judgment sound, only two peoples are sure of still being there—the Chinese . . . and us!

And all along this laborious path of "survival," one absence until very recently always seemed to us to be particularly conspicuous and quite incomprehensible: that of

France. For two centuries, emphasized rather than diminished by our communal participation in two world wars, there was between us a trench of ignorance and mistrust which our periodic relations succeeded only in digging deeper.

So it isn't excessive, or at least a little so, that we should say: "At last de Gaulle came. . . ." And this was not only, nor even particularly for his prophetic "Vive le Québec libre!" which resounded all around the world. One must remember that well before, in 1961 with Premier Lesage, the general had wanted to preside over a real reacquaintance between France and Quebec and, doubtless driven by his passion for the old country and what it had produced that was most durable, he went to the trouble of studying the information on the unique offspring that we are. And I can tell you that he knew this information intimately, better than anyone other than the interested principals.

His knowledge was absolutely perfect. It was not only that of the "Canadiens" of the ancient regime, nor only that of the French Canadians of yesteryear. But also that of the Quebecers as we were then beginning to call ourselves more and more. During the 1960s, following a maturing of which nobody had taken too much notice, it was Quebec which emerged briskly, Quebec alone, and no longer the "province of Quebec," interior colony of federal Canada. It emerged moreover without hostility, without the slightest intentions of revenge, which simply indicated that along the way to self-determination, the hour of self-affirmation had sounded.

To this rapid awakening, which we were ourselves the first to find astonishing, we have given the name the "quiet revolution," which was not ill-founded. Revolutionary it certainly was, if one accepts that a fundamental change can happen without killings and ruins. Quiet, and in consequence marked by a continuity in change, even in the most radical change, which is one of the characteristics of our people. Quietly therefore, but on all levels we saw a liberation which was as sudden as is the breaking of the icepacks on our rivers in the spring. And the ground began to flower and to produce like never before: reform as profound as it was late in the field of education; the initiation of a modern administration, so well organized that it shows signs of a bureaucratic fat which is not exclusively French—but also a jump in social awareness which, on several major points moved rapidly from the back to the foreground; and an increasingly keen consciousness of responsibilities such as the essentials of economic life.

And as is usual, all this was announced by and accompanied by artists, an unprecedented plethora of writers, painters, film-makers, architects, and in particular some superb popular poets, several of whom are well-known in France, who have created for us a repertory of songs which are reminiscent of your old provincial airs that rocked us in our cradles, and in which we now find our own countenance and our accents of today, and a precise echo of our successes, our failures, and our plans. It is this new, renewed Quebec which de Gaulle took the trouble to see. Contrary to what some people have thought, he did not have to "invent" it.

Inevitably this metamorphosis owed it to itself to create an instrument for its political expression and to try to conduct it to its logical conclusion. This instrument is the Parti Québécois. We were just a few hundred, then a few thousand, to bring it into being in 1967–68, with two objectives which have remained coupled since then: sovereignty and association. This means a sovereign State of Quebec which will accept, or rather offer in advance, new links of interdependence with Canada, but links which will this time be negotiated between equal peoples, as a function of their geographic and other unquestionable common interests.

These two objectives, which may seem contradictory, are in reality perfectly complimentary; and if they involve a risk this also seems to us as logical today as ten years ago when we were doing it for the first time, when we forsaw all these refusals with which we would always, contrary to good sense, be faced. In the face of any change which disturbs, even when one knows in one's heart that it will be necessary for it to happen, the first reaction of the established order is infallibly negative. First, and for as long as possible they always say "No." Like King Canute trying to stop the sea. . . .

This, briefly, is the national option, inscribed from the beginning in the heart of a political program in which each paragraph, each word, has been rigorously exposed to the attention of every Quebecer. But like anyone else, certainly, over and above these existential but not very day-to-day questions which we are resolving—for a while—in the Constitution, our people are also experiencing all the problems, the frustrations and the hopes of the men and women of their time. This is why, on the way, we must also try to respond the best we can, with the power the federal regime deigns to give us, to these requirements of our citizens.

To the overall plan of society that we have attempted to describe, others have given a European name tag: that of social democracy. It sometimes seems to me to be preferable to talk, with no qualification, simply of democracy, that old ideal which we never completely attain but which we must pursue persistently in order to install it as far as we can in all those areas of life where it is still so greatly in default: in housing as in business, with the old as with the young, with women, with consumers, with those whom prosperity has left behind, but first and foremost, and with a special determination, in political activity. Electoral rights belong to citizens only. It is therefore not right—and we have determined this by law—to allow companies, or unions, or any "pressure group", to meddle financially in the parties. For us, in our situation, this is a basic requirement. And if real democracy is to be established everywhere it is necessary for a society which is interested in this task to have full and complete liberty to do so in its own fashion, according to its priorities. It is this need for liberty—the best synonym for which, in my humble opinion is responsibility—which explains to a very large degree our objective of national independence. Whether it is a question of management of the land, of social security or of economic progress, interaction is such in the modern world that one cannot conduct coherent and effective policies if one holds only fractions of power and portions of fiscal resources. This calls for legislative and financial means that Quebec does not currently possess and which it can find only through the acquisition of sovereignty.

But there is, in addition, the constant, pressing, daily worry of maintaining a linguistic and cultural identity which has lost the old security of an isolated, rural and prolific Quebec, an identity which is today exposed as never before to the major transcontinental influences of the American culture, and which risks, in addition, being swamped by the immigration policy of a federal state which we will never control, and by the excessive weight in Quebec of an anglophone minority, the managing circles, which have exercised a truly colonialist influence for too long. This identity, after almost four hundred years, is so much a part of the intrinsic soul of Quebec that, without it, it would no longer have any reason to be.

Furthermore, while awaiting the definitive security which only our own political institutions will be able to guarantee us, we became, in the first months of our mandate, the third Quebec government in a row to see itself obliged to propose a bill for the defense and promotion of a language which, under normal circumstances, would never have needed such artificial aid.

This is why, in a referendum which will be held before the next elections, and which, obviously, will involve only ourselves, the option of a sovereign Quebec, political master of its entire internal life and its future, will be proposed. To which there is nothing to prevent adding the complementary offer which I mentioned previously, which is that of negotiating with Canada an association that will be essentially economic, and that will be not only as profitable for Canada as for ourselves but also no less necessary to its continuity.

Whatever happens, Canada as a whole now knows,

almost as well as Quebec, that at the very least some profound changes are required. The constitutional regime conceded to a handful of colonies in the last century has become a pillory. Behind the fiction of the ten provinces, two distinct peoples, who both have the same right to self-determination, find themselves not only cramped, but in increasing danger of each poisoning the other, like the two scorpions which Churchill described, locked into the same bottle. For a quarter of a century now an evolving Quebec has posed its question with constantly increasing insistence. They have evaded it as far as they can. But we have now arrived at a point where, stage by stage, agreement is in the process of being reached on the necessity for a political renewal. Instead of yet another bad compromise, the rational association of two peoples and two states which we propose seems to us to be the only means of assuring, for both sides, a more harmonious and infinitely more stimulating future. This is not a question of destroying something that is already condemned, but of beginning, together, to build something realistic, noble and eminently fruitful.

For us Quebecers, this is literally a question of our right to live.

And this demand does not only seem to us to be natural and normal, which it obviously is, but also very clearly inscribed in a universal movement. In spite of the risk of new hegemonies, in spite of the risk of the domestication of spirits, of the folkloring of cultures, the real chance for a new, world-wide humanism must arrive through the original and constructive contribution of nationals, which we are. In America, where we have been holding our small fort for so long, our success or failure will in a way announce that of other peoples who are also at grips with the struggle and the rage to live, and who are also searching for their path.

For France and for the future of the French language and culture, it cannot be a matter of indifference whether, on this other continent, a free people should have the liberty to express in French, but in its own accent, every dimension of today's world.

As Quebec—which will have the eleventh highest per capita income of more than a hundred and fifty countries, and whose human and material resources promise a future to which only our wills can set the limits—as Quebec is strong and self assured, so France and the French-speaking world will be increasingly strengthened.

Like any other normal people Quebecers will soon have to decide among themselves their preferred political status and their national future. Given all that unites us, we are hoping that we will receive from you, and from all francophones, both understanding and sympathy. Whatever happens we expect to maintain and to increase, with your people, on a basis of equality, a special relationship which will be mutually fruitful and advantageous in every respect.

René Lévesque
(Speech to the members of the French National Assembly, November 2, 1977)

Appendices

Appendix 1

From Nouvelle-France
to a Sovereign Quebec

I From Jacques Cartier to the Act of Union

1. Nouvelle-France (1534-1763)

1534   Jacques Cartier, from St. Malo, disembarks in the Gaspé, on the eastern point of Quebec, and takes possession of the land in the name of Francis I.

1604   Settling of French pioneers on the banks of the St. Lawrence.

1608   Founding of Quebec, on the site of an Indian village, by Samuel de Champlain, cartographer for Sgr. De Monts, named by the King lieutenant-general of Nouvelle-France.

1615–   Voyage of exploration up the St. Lawrence as far as Lake
1616   Ontario.

1634   Founding of Trois-Rivières.

1642   Founding of Ville-Marie, the future Montreal, by Paul de Chomeday de Maisonneuve, near the Indian village of Hochelaga.

1663   Nouvelle-France becomes a royal colony.

1674   Creation of the bishopric of Quebec, the first incumbant being Mgr. de Laval.

1713   Treaty of Utrecht after the War of the Spanish Succession. Newfoundland and Acadia ceded to the English.

1734   Opening of the main road, the "chemin du Roy" between Quebec and Montreal.

1755   Deportation of Acadians from Nova Scotia by the English Army.

1759   Siege of Quebec and defeat of French armies. General de Montcalm and General Wolfe killed in battle on the Plains of Abraham, and the foot of the fortress of Quebec.

2. The English Regime (1763–1840)

1763   Signing of the Treaty of Paris. Nouvelle-France becomes the English colony of Canada. The "royal proclamation" of King George III abolishes free exercise of the Catholic religion and establishes English civil and criminal laws.

1764   Publication of the *Gazette du Québec,* a bilingual newspaper which disappeared in 1842.

1773– England lessens its hold on Quebec in order to better resist
1774   the American movement for independence.

1774   Quebec Act: French civil law re-established, "free exercise of the religion of the church of Rome" is assured. Beginning of the uprising of the thirteen American colonies with the Philadelphia Declaration of Rights.

1776   Declaration of Independence by the American colonies. A first military invasion by America is repulsed.

1783   Treaty of Versailles: end of the Anglo-American war. Many American loyalists settle in the Ontario region.

1791   The Constitutional Act is voted in London. Canada divided into two provinces, Upper Canada (10,000 inhabitants, anglophone) and Lower Canada (150,000 inhabitants, francophone), with identical institutions: a government, an Assembly and Executive Council.

1792   The *parti canadien démocratique* (French speaking) totally disregards the British rules of parliamentarianism and dominates the Assembly. The English Party applies to London to unite the two provinces. Situation worsens culminating in 1837 with revolt by Papineau.

1793   Debate on the language question in the Quebec house.

1804   Napoleon I.

1806– Censorship of newspaper *Le Canadien.* Its proprietors and
1810   editors thrown in prison.

1812   War between United States and England: second American military invasion of Canada.

1817   Creation of the Bank of Montreal.

1822   Proposal for the union of the two Canadas. Proposed text prescribes use of French in the legislature.

1823 Monroe Doctrine "America for the Americans." Charles X, King of France; George IV, King of England.

1829 Founding of McGill University in Montreal.

1831 Alexis de Tocqueville's journey to Canada. Louis Philippe, King of the French.

1836 Opening of the first railway line.
Victoria, Queen of England.

1837– Louis-Joseph Papineau, chief of the *parti-patriote*, fights for
1838 representative government based on popular sovereignty, and on ministerial responsibility, and for the rights of Canadian nationalism in the face of the British governor. Instigates a rebellion in the two provinces. L.J. Papineau is exiled. Twelve patriots hanged in Montreal.

1839 Lord Durham's report on the state of Canada after the 1837–38 rebellion. He advises the anglicization of the francophones and the establishment of responsible government.

1840 Act of Union: English law unites the two provinces into one single colony. The Chamber is composed of the same number of representatives for Upper Canada (450,000 inhabitants) as for Lower Canada (650,000 inhabitants). Regime generates tension within francophone population who feel under-represented and wronged: debts are shared *per capita* across the population, although Ontario's debts are much greater than those of Quebec. English declared sole official language.

II From Union to the "quiet revolution"

1. Birth of Canada 1840–1867

1840– Campaigns favoring colonization, to prevent massive
1850 emigration of francophones to the United States. Forty thousand leave during this period.

1848 Recognition of equality of the two official languages. French and English.

1850– Impasse in United Canada. From 1858 no government is
1867 sure of a stable majority. Confrontation between East and West.

1851 Census indicates that for the first time francophones are less numerous than anglophones.

1852 Founding of Laval University, in Quebec.

1855 Franco-Quebec reconciliation on the occasion of the visit of the *Capricieuse*.

1859 Creation of a French consulate in Quebec.

1862 England withdraws troops from Canada.

1864 Napoleon III.

1866 Reunion in London of representatives of United Canada, New Brunswick and Nova Scotia.

1867 The British North America Act is passed, creating a confederation, the Dominion of Canada, with four provinces: Ontario, Quebec, Nova Scotia, New Brunswick. French has the status of official language in Parliaments in Ottawa and Quebec and before federal and Quebec courts.

2. First Years of Confederation

Period marked by the development of agriculture, with moves towards dairy farming. Developing industry faces shortage of capital, and runs against a society more rural than urban. Expansion of the power of the clergy and tension between Ottawa and Quebec.

1869 Louis Riel, leading the Métis Indians, forms a provincial government in western Ontario. Trouble breaks out. Louis Riel flees to the United States.

1870 Manitoba becomes fifth province of Canada. Has bilingual status similar to that of Quebec.
New Brunswick abolishes Catholic schools (francophone).

1871 Entry of British Columbia into the Dominion.

1875 Creation of the Supreme Court of Canada.

1880 From this date until 1910, intense period of correspondence and economic collaboration between France and Quebec.

1881 Journey of Quebec prime minister, Chapleau to Paris, where he is received by Gambetta, president of the *Conseil Français*.

1882 Opening of *Agence générale du Québec* in France.

1885 Another Métis (francophone) revolt. Hanging of Louis Riel provokes violent reaction in Quebec, which is preoccupied with struggles for linguistic and educational rights of francophones living outside Quebec.

1887 Honoré Mercier, prime minister of Quebec, calls the first Prime Ministers' Conference in order to resist the centralizing tendencies of the government of the Dominion.

1889 Closing of French schools in Manitoba.

1891 President of the French Republic, Sadi Carnot, receives Honoré Mercier in Paris.

1896 Wilfrid Laurier, leader of the federal Liberal party becomes prime minister of the Dominion, with massive Quebec support. He is the first francophone to hold this post.

1897 Creation of a free-trade area between Great Britain and the dominions.

1900– Beginnings of industrialization in Quebec. Quebecers
1910 protest Canada's participation in England's colonial wars.

1901 Canadian trade unions decide to continue to be affiliated with American federations.

1905 Alberta and Saskatchewan enter the Canadian confederation.

3. Quebec and the First World War (1910-1920)

1910 George V, King of Great Britain.
Henri Bourassa founds *Le Devoir,* Quebec daily newspaper.

1912 Official termination of franco-Quebec relations.

1914 Declaration of war. Canada offers troops to England. Protests in Quebec: "If they ask us to fight for England, we will reply 'When we have our schools back!'"

1915 Restriction on the use of French in Ontario.

1917 Military service becomes obligatory. Pacifist demonstrations in Quebec and Montreal against conscription. Bloody repression, "Motion Francoeur" presented in the House: "that this House is of the opinion that the Province of Quebec would be disposed to accept the breaking of the federal pact of 1867 if, in other provinces, it is believed that it is an obstacle to the union, progress and development of Canada."

4. Canada on the International Scene (1920-1945)

Government favors massive investment in the Ontario industrial infrastructure and reduces Quebecers to the state of highly favored pensioners. The masses urbanise. Traditional elites are replaced. A working class is formed.

1918   Disturbances in Quebec.

1920   Creation of the University of Montreal.

1931   Statute of Westminster: international status accorded to the Dominions. Canada thus obtains independence.

1934   Election of Maurice Duplessis, leader of the *Union nationale* (the Conservative party), as Prime Minister of Quebec.

1937   The King's Privy Council in London, acting as Canada's constitutional court, refuses the government of the Dominion the right to enforce treaties it has signed with international organizations if the measures it would be required to take fall into domains which the British North America Act designated as the exclusive responsibility of the governments of the provinces. Quebec demands a decentralization of power and opposes Ottawa's right to enquire into provincial finances.

1939-   Liberal party in power during the Second World War. Takes
1944   advantage of the war to partially nationalize the hydro-electric system and create Hydro-Quebec (1944).

5. The Duplessis Reign (1946-1959)

Under the Duplessis administration, Quebec becomes industrialized but the workers conflicts become larger and more violent.

Quebec undergoes an artistic awakening with the Rideau-Vert theatre (1948), les jeunesses musicales (1949), the art gallery of Agnes Lefort (1950), the Nouveau-Monde theatre (1951) and the Comédie-Canadienne (1958). The grand-prix du Disque is awarded to Félix Leclerc (1951). Authors include Anne Hébert, Marcel Dubé. Noteworthy magazines appear: *Cité libre* (1950), *Liberté* (1958), *La Revue socialiste* (1959).

Maurice Duplessis fights against decentralization in Ottawa and the fiscal powers of the central government. Principal themes of "Duplessism": provincial autonomy, private enterprise, struggle against the unions.

1948   Quebec asbestos strike.
       Adoption of the Quebec flag.

1949   Entry of Newfoundland into the dominion, after a referendum.

1952   Elizabeth II

Abolition of recourse to the judiciary committee of the Queen's Privy Council, in London as supreme court of appeal for Canada.

Inauguration of the first television station in Montreal.

Reintroduction of income tax in Quebec.

1954   Creation of Sherbrooke University.

1956   In Ottawa, Liberal Cabinet under Louis Saint-Laurent. René Lévesque accompanies Mr. Lester B. Pearson, federal minister of foreign affairs, on a visit to the world's capitals, including Moscow.

Beginning of René Lévesque's program "Point de Mire."

1957   Election of conservative John Diefenbaker to head the federal government.

1958   December, beginning of the long strike at Radio-Canada.

1959   Opening of the St. Lawrence Seaway, opening the Atlantic to the Great Lakes.

Death of Maurice Duplessis in Schefferville.

Paul Sauvé succeeds him for a hundred days. A leitmotiv: "Henceforth..., "

III   From the "quiet revolution" to René Lévesque's victory

1. The "quiet revolution" (1960–1967)

Quebec youth and the intellectuals favor Jean Lesage's reforms. The clergy makes itself discreet and in some cases support these reforms. The fashionable authors are Gérard Bessette, Gratien Gélinas, Paul Chamberland, Jacques Renaud, Hubert Aquin, Rejean Ducharme, Jacques Godbout, Michel Tremblay, Pierre Vallières, Roch Carrier, Yves Thériault. Magazines and newspapers in which ideas are exchanged appear: *Recherches Sociographiques, les Écrits du Canada français, Maintenant, Cité libre, Liberté, Parti pris, Socialisme, Études françaises, La Barre du jour, Culture vivante, Québec Presse, Point de Mire, Le Nouveau journal, Mainmise*. Between 1961 and 1965 traditional Quebec society is questioned, the predominance of the clergy, electoral corruption, economic backwardness, deficiencies in matters of language and education. However, the hopes unleashed by the liberals end in confrontation among the workers and on an ideological level.

1960   *June:* Victory of provincial Liberal party—then national-istic—in Quebec. Slogan: "It's time for change." Under the name of the "quiet revolution," the new provincial Prime Minister, Jean Lesage, plunges into a policy of emancipation.

1961   *Feb.:* Creation of the Royal Commission of Enquiry into Teaching, the so-called "Parent Commission." On walls in Quebec is written "Down with Confederation!"

       March: Creation of ministry of cultural affairs and ministry of resources (Energy and Mines). René Lévesque is the first to hold the portfolio.

       Oct.: General de Gaulle receives Jean Lesage on an official visit. Quebec opens a general delegation in Paris.

1962   *Nov.:* Quebec electors return the Liberals to power and approve the principle of the nationalization of hydroelectric-ity. Slogan: "Masters in our own home."

1963   *March:* First bombs by Quebec Liberation Front (F.L.Q.)

       April: Federal Liberal party wins elections. Lester Pearson Prime Minister of Canada, and remains so after losing his absolute majority in 1965.

1964   *Jan.:* General de Gaulle receives Lester Pearson in an official visit. While underlining the "special and natural closeness" of France and Quebec, he declares that nothing can damage "excellent franco-Canadian relations."

       Feb.: Authors of the preliminary report of the Commission of Enquiry on Bilingualism and Biculturalism affirm that Canada is going through the most critical period in its history. First international agreement signed in Paris by the Quebec provincial government. This agreement relates to franco-Quebec co-operation in the field of education.

       March: Creation of the Ministry of Education.

       Oct.: Visit by the Queen. Police intervene and club separatist demonstrators.

       Nov.: Signing of another franco-Quebec agreement on culture.

Dec.: After thirty-three days of debates the House of Commons in Ottawa adopts a Canadian flag.

1965 *Jan.:* French government officially recognizes the Quebec delegation in Paris.
Arrest in New York of Pierre Vallières, who will go to prison and write *Nègres blancs d'Amérique.*

1966 *June:* Liberals become unpopular.
Reformed *Union nationale* wins elections in Quebec. Daniel Johnson, nationalist, becomes Prime Minister and introduces the slogan: "Equality or Independence."

1967 *April:* Creation of Ministry of Intergovernmental Affairs.
Centenary of the Confederation of Canada and opening of the World Fair in Montreal.

May: Daniel Johnson makes official visit to France. General de Gaulle calls him: "My friend, Daniel Johnson. . . ."

July: Invited by the federal and Quebec governments (for Montreal Expo), General de Gaulle ends a speech on July 24, in Montreal, with his notorious "Vive le Québec libre!" Following a protest by the Canadian government, he cancels his visit to Ottawa.

An historical point: Vive le Québec libre

During a conference organized by the Charles de Gaulle Institute, many comments were made on the notorious "Vive le Québec libre!" uttered by de Gaulle in Montreal in July 1967.

The former secretary general to the President of the Republic, M. Burin des Rosiers, was very clear: "The exclamation was not premeditated. De Gaulle felt compelled to respond to the crowds who had continually acclaimed him on his journey along the "chemin du Roy." The unnumerable placards brandished, reading 'France libre, Québec libre,' must have impressed themselves on his mind."

M. Pérol, former press advisor to the President of the Republic, remarked: "De Gaulle always prepared all his official speeches with great care. He never wrote this phrase. He nevertheless admitted to its paternity in his press conference on the following November 27."

M. de Saint-Léger, former diplomatic advisor at the Elysée Palace, considered that it was an "historical phenomenon" generated by political climate of the time. He recalled that several hours later de Gaulle had added: "What I did, I had to do."

With regard to Canada, M. de Saint Leger added, de Gaulle had "no feelings of enmity." He had first of all assessed that Quebec could conserve its own personality within the federal framework, but he had then come to think that it should be "a sovereign state, freely able to determine its relationship with its neighboring sovereign state, which would be negotiated to preserve Canada."

The English journalist Harold King recalled in this respect that de Gaulle had assured him that he was not aiming for "the breaking up of Canadian unity."

Sept.: Official signature of two agreements (education and culture) in Paris by M. Alain Peyrefitte and Daniel Johnson.

Oct.: René Lévesque leaves the Liberal party and founds the Sovereignty-Association Movement.

2. Development of the Parti Québécois (1968–1970)

1968   Assassination of Martin Luther King and Robert Kennedy. May troubles in France. USSR invades Prague. Creation of franco-Quebec office for youth.

April: In Ottawa, Mr. Pearson cedes his place to Montrealer Pierre Elliott Trudeau, who wants to introduce "bilingualism" across Canada.

June: P.E. Trudeau faces rioting crowd on Saint-Jean Baptiste Day.

Sept.: Daniel Johnson dies suddenly on the eve of another official visit to France. Succeeded by Mr. Jacques Bertrand. Crucial problem: the language question.

Oct.: Formation of René Lévesque's Parti Québécois, which absorbs the small independentist movements.

Nov.: Formation of ministry of immigration.

1969   *July:* Increasing number of riots and bombs as politicians in office adopt an increasing number of anti-democratic measures vis-à-vis francophones. French becomes official language in all federal Canadian institutions.

April: Liberal party, led by Robert Bourassa, wins elections on platform of maintaining Canadian federation. René Lévesque loses his seat. Violence breaks out.

Oct.-Dec.: Mr. James Cross, head of the British Trade Commission in Montreal, and subsequently Pierre Laporte, Quebec Minister of Labour and Manpower, kidnapped by the Quebec Liberation Front October 17. "War Measures" are brought into force by P. E. Trudeau who imprisons all those opposing his federalist ideas. According to certain information received, this violence was remote controlled by the RCMP in the service of the politicians in power. Pierre Laporte is found, assassinated. Mr. James Cross is freed, safe and sound, December 3. The FLQ is declared outlawed. René Lévesque declares: "Those who coldly executed Mr. Laporte,

having seen him live and hope for so many days, are
inhuman.

3. The irresistable rise of the Parti Québécois (1971–1976)

Art and literature revive the strength of the silenced opposition
forces, with Pierre Vadeboncoeur, Françoise Loranger, Gaston
Miron, Gilles Vigneault, Georges Dor, Robert Charlebois, Denys
Arcand, Michel Brault, Claude Jutra.

1971   *June:* The Bourassa government rejects as insufficient a bill
       for the reform of the Canadian federation put forward in
       Victoria.

       Oct.: Violent demonstrations in Quebec following the
       closure of the newspaper *La Presse,* the principal French
       language newspaper in Montreal.

       Dec.: Creation of the James Bay Development Company,
       whose objective is to develop and exploit the riches of the
       region, with special priority to Quebec interests.

1972   *Oct.:* M. Trudeau loses his absolute majority in the federal
       elections. He remains at the head of a minority government.
       General strike in Quebec of 210,000 unionized workers in
       the public and parapublic sectors. Repercussions affect
       unionists in the private sector, who are affiliated to the three
       large centrals. The leaders of the three centrals are
       imprisoned for contempt of court.

       Dec.: Robert Bourassa formulates his policy of "cultural
       independence within economic federalism."

1973   *Oct.:* Bourassa increases his majority. The Liberal party wins
       100 out of 108 seats. The *Union nationale* collapses and is no
       longer represented in the House. The Parti Québécois (6
       seats but 30 per cent of the vote) becomes the official
       opposition party.

1974   *May:* The Bourassa government adopts "Law 22," institut-
       ing French as the sole official language in Quebec.

       Oct.: Official visit to France—the first for ten years—by the
       Canadian Prime Minister, M. Trudeau.

       Dec.: Official visit to France by the Quebec Premier, M.
       Bourassa.

1976   *Oct.:* M. Bourassa decides to call provincial elections.

       15 Nov.: The Parti Québécois wins a resounding victory.

Appendix 2

Distribution of the Francophone Population in Canada

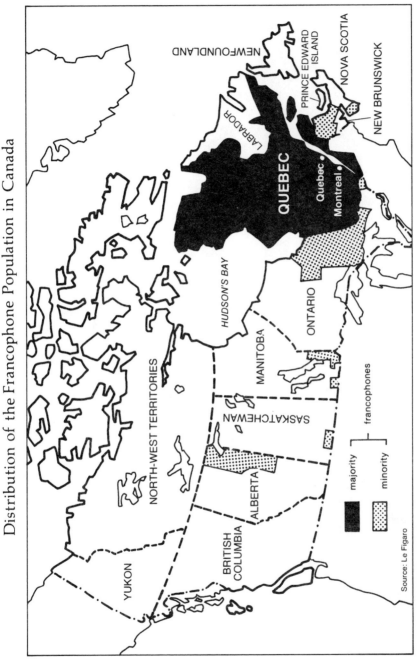

Source: Le Figaro

Appendix 3

The French Language Charter

French—I know it by heart.
(Campaign for the recognition of French conducted by the Télé-Université of Quebec.)

On August 26, 1977, the French Language Charter made French the official language of Quebec (Law 101). This Charter supersedes Law 22 on the official language, which had been in force since July 31, 1974.

Fundamental rights

In addition to affirming that French is the official language of Quebec, the law recognizes certain fundamental linguistic rights; it decrees that:

— every person has the right that the Administration, the health services, the social services, the public utilities, professional groups, salaried workers' associations, and the various businesses operating in Quebec, should communicate with him/her in French;
— in a deliberating assembly, every person has the right to express him/herself in French;
— workers have the right to carry out their activities in French;
— consumers of goods or services have the right to be informed and served in French;
— every person admitted to a course of learning in Quebec has the right to receive this learning in French.

French as the language of work

In the chapter on the language of work, the Charter makes French the official language to be used in working relationships, and requires the employer to draw up in French all communications addressed to employees, including both offers of work and of promotion.

French as the language of business and commerce

From July 3, 1978 any label on a product, on its content or on its packaging, on a document or on an object accompanying this product, including method of use, and certificates of guarantee, and all menus and wine lists must be drawn up in French.

French as the language of teaching

The Charter decrees that the teaching must be in French, in kindergartens, and in primary and secondary schools in Quebec.

The following may be taught in English at the request of their mother and their father:

— children whose father or mother received his or her primary education in English in Quebec;
— children whose father or mother was, on August 26, 1977, resident in Quebec and who received his or her primary education, outside Quebec, in English;
— children who, during the school year immediately preceding August 26, 1977, legally received, in Quebec, their teaching in English in a public kindergarten or in a primary or secondary school.
— the younger brothers and sisters of the above.

One of the major objectives of the Charter is indisputably the francisation of businesses. This operation consists of making the use of French general in all companies conducting business in Quebec.

Every company employing fifty or more persons must, by December 31, 1983, possess a certificate of francisation issued by the French Language Office. This certificate testifies that the business is applying a program of francisation whose objectives comprise: knowledge of the official language by managers; an increase at all levels of the business of the number of persons having a good knowledge of French, and the utilization of French as the language of work and internal communications.

The more happens in Quebec,
the more it happens in French.
(Télé-Université of Quebec)

Appendix 4

Quebec Culture

Extracts from the White Paper
on Cultural Development (June 1978)

A visitor to Quebec cannot immediately detect signs of a specific
and truly original cultural entity. The casual observer is even
tempted to conclude that Quebecers have invented very little and
that their claim to cultural originality is based on a vast body of
borrowings rather than the confluence of typically *québécois*
creations. He quickly perceives for instance that the language and
civil law are of French origin; a certain ability to live close to nature
derives from the Amerindian culture; the political institutions and
criminal law come from Britain; the Roman Catholic faith is at the
origin of religious thought and institutions; the economic and
industrial structures and the technology are borrowed from the
United States.

Even a short stay in Quebec is sufficient to convince a visitor that
when he crossed the border, although his eyes distinguished no
difference with Ontario or the United States, he entered another
socio-cultural world. The difference, as we shall again mention
further on, is not due simply to the presence of French Quebecers,
although that is an important factor: you need only listen to and
speak with these Quebecers to discover preoccupations, aspirations, hopes, worries and anxieties that have scarcely an equivalent
anywhere else in the world. You will also hear of a distinct identity,
of survival, of a specific patrimony, of a determination to preserve a
language and certain values, of a country to be built, of great spaces
to be conquered, of dignity and pride, of devotion to the land.

If democracy is to develop its full potential, it must extend beyond
the political, social and economic system to become cultural. And if
his right to his culture is to mean anything, a citizen must have free
and easy access to all cultural property, in spite of geographic,
economic and social restrictions. He must be able to use the
resources of the community to develop his own talents and creative
potential. And finally he must be able to join with those around him
whenever he chooses, in whatever community he may find himself,

in the development of a vibrant culture which expresses both his identity and his free choice.

The cultural situation in Quebec is not that of an independent people. The incorporation of this community into the Canadian federation, which sometimes claims to be a "nation", imposes special limitations on Quebec which become shackles when it attempts to develop its own values and cultural endeavours. It feels restricted in ways of which it is not always aware, and exposed to temptations to which it sometimes succumbs. The most common and at the same time most notable of those temptations is that of catering to "Culture" and not to human beings.

There are large non-Francophone minorities in Quebec, particularly in Montreal. There is no more question of ignoring this diversity, which will be dealt with in greater detail in subsequent chapters, than there is of ignoring the different social classes and regions found in a territory the size of Quebec. Yet, without ignoring the diversity of these cultural sources, is it possible to determine a focal point for them all?

The reactions to the Charter of the French language have been very revealing in this respect. Even the Charter's most adamant opponents have admitted that French should without question be the common language of Quebec. In other words, even if English, Italian and Greek can and should be freely spoken in Quebec, everyone should at least be able to communicate by means of one common language. But the logical consequences must be accepted. A language is not simply syntax or a string of words. It is an expression of the more meaningful aspects of community life.

If French is to be Quebec's common language, as everyone seems to agree, then the cultural consequences must be accepted. Not, let it be repeated, because the French tradition must drive all others out of Quebec, but because the French culture, like the French language, should serve as a *focal point* for the various communities which will continue to make their presence felt and to express their own cultural values.

The government is as anxious to promote contact between the minorities and the culture of the French majority by every possible means as it is to respect and contribute to their development.

Between slow or brusque assimilation, and preservation of original characteristics confined within the walls of segregation, there is another practicable road, that of exchanges within a Quebec culture. In the course of everyday life, in a city like Montreal, for example, mutual exchanges and borrowing have long been the order of the day. Often these take place with the utmost simplicity, sometimes they require great effort. It is important to work more openly in this direction.

Obviously, unless relations between francophone Quebecers and Quebecers of other origins are transformed, we cannot really talk of a common project. The cultural vitality of the minorities has already exerted a profound influence on Quebec life. We have dealt at length with the many contributions of the English community and its varied institutions. We must also consider the pioneer work done in the health and welfare sector by the Jewish people, the contributions made in the housing field by the Italians, the renewal of the Saint-Louis district of Montreal by the Portuguese, the multiplicity of jobs and business firms created by so many Quebecers of foreign origins. These are only a few examples gleaned in passing; there is no question of drawing up an honors list. Aside from these visible achievements, and many others, there are intangible assets: the sense of the value of work, the sense of responsibility and the sense of community. Such values have helped and will continue to help build Quebec.

Appendix 5

Federal Evangelism

The constitutional law which governs the relationship between the federal parliament in Ottawa and the provincial assemblies (including, therefore Quebec) was voted by the British Parliament in 1867. This law is known as the British North America Act. Any modification to this Act must be decided by London. Periodically, therefore, the question of repatriating the constitution arises.

. . . Provincial interests and the interests of Canada's two linguistic groups are not and cannot be represented simply through the device of transferring powers from the federal government to the provincial governments. . . .

. . . The division of powers between orders of government should be guided by principles of functionalism, and not by ethnic considerations. . . .

. . . The Parliament of Canada must have responsibility for the major and inextricably inter-related instruments of economic policy if it is to stimulate employment and control inflation. It must have control over monetary and credit policy, the balance-wheel role in fiscal policy, tariff policy, and balance of payments policy. It must be responsible for interprovincial and international trade. It must be able to undertake measures for stimulating the growth of the economy some of which inevitably and some of which intentionally will affect regional economic growth. . . .

. . . The government of Canada must have the power to redistribute income, between persons and between provinces. This would involve, as it does now, the rights to make payments to individuals, for the purpose of supporting their income levels—old age security pensions, unemployment insurance, family allowances. . . .

. . . The government of Canada believes it must be able to speak for Canada, internationally, and that it must be able to act for Canada in strengthening the bonds of nationhood. . . . This seems to us to imply an active federal role in the cultural and technological developments which so characterize the twentieth century. We acknowledge, of course, that the nourishment of Canada's cultural diversity requires imaginative provincial programmes as well as federal ones.

(Extracts from the White Paper published by Ottawa in 1968, entitled: *Federalism for the Future. A Statement of Policy by the Government of Canada.*)

Source: Claude Morin, Le Combat québécois (Boréal Express, 1973)

Appendix 6
Road and Rail Map of Canada

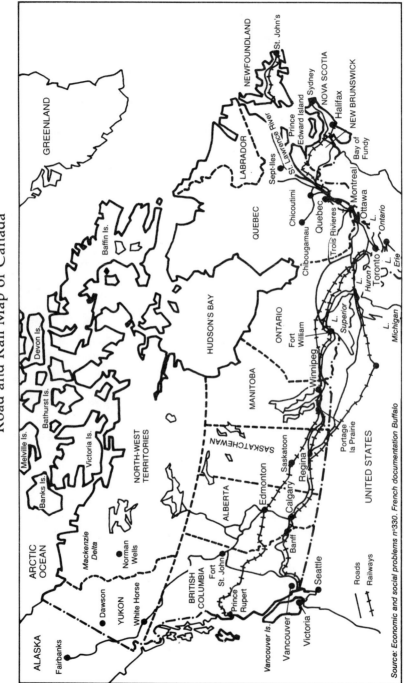

Source: Economic and social problems n°330. French documentation Buffalo

Addendum, February 1979

*During your speech to the First Ministers' Conference on the Constitution
in October 1978 there was a suggestion that Quebec's independence is the
inevitable outcome of history. On what evidence is this based? Could it not
be that the reverse is equally true—that the inevitable outcome is more
active participation in the Canadian political scene?*

Certainly it could happen that way also. But to me, it would be
a sort of national abortion. I do believe that, in due time, and
hopefully very soon, the currents of evolution, are bound to
bring the Quebec people to self-government. Our whole
history, with the slow and laborious but uninterrupted
political development that marked it, points in that direction:
from a French colony with a strong North American identity,
through "survival" after the Conquest, then our share of
responsible government, to a "half-state" with provincial
status, and now to the deep crisis in Quebec—Canada's
institutional links. A crisis which the Pépin-Robarts Report
very clear-mindedly ties to "duality", the basic question posed
by the coexistence of two different national entities. There is
the Gordian knot that has to be untied. The only way is
through recognition of the full equality of two peoples. And
that is quite obviously the way in which public opinion in
Quebec has come to see the future. Especially as the new
generations come of age. So in a democratic context, I really
think the conclusion is bound to be something like what we
propose.

During that same conference you suggested that you would not give your agreement to patriation of the British North America Act despite the urging of Prime Minister Trudeau. He suggested that this would maintain Canada in a colonial position. Why did you disagree? What would it take to change your mind?

As provincial Premier, playing the game according to present rules and traditional Quebec positions, I could not and will not accept any "patriation" unless and until a new division of powers has been established. All we had in front of us, in the 78-79 round of conferences, was a so-called "short list" of basically insignificant constitutional proposals established unilaterally by the Feds. And even on such a meagre diet, except for one item, there was no consensus! Accepting patriation under such circumstances, along with its logical complement of an amending formula, would simply risk fixing the status quo in constitutional cement. For as long as we are exposed to remaining in a Federal system, we are betraying all of Quebec's aspirations and its needs for fundamental change.

As for Mr. Trudeau's argument about the "colonial" position in which trips to Westminster keep us, it's rather comical. All he wants is a symbolic feather in his cap as patriator of an old and quite obsolete imperial text. What an up-to-date federalist should be proposing is a brand new set of institutions made in Canada. . . .

What would your reaction be to Mr. Trudeau patriating the constitution unilaterally over your expressed objection? Do you think he can do this?

I'm not sure he could. In fact, apart from some aspects that are strictly in the Federal field of competence, I'm pretty sure he couldn't, without running into more trouble than an old and rather run-down government could cope with.

Recently there was an announcement that your government was planning to become more actively involved in the asbestos industry. What do you plan to do with it?

I've explained the basic reasons for our asbestos policy in the book: a share in ownership (somewhat comparable to Saskatchewan's potash policy), market know-how, job creation, etc. To bring you up to date, let me just add that, after long and detailed evaluation by both sides, we are for the moment unable to come to an agreed purchase price with the controlling interest in Asbestos Corporation, the company we have decided to bring under Quebec ownership. If this goes on, we are ready to pass an expropriation Bill, with arbitration, recourse to courts and all the normal equitable practices for such an operation.

Could you describe the energy policy of an independent Quebec?

Here again, I believe you get a pretty complete description in the book. It is based on a White Paper on energy which we published in 1978. In a nutshell, it simply emphasizes the fact that, like almost everyone else in the world, we're going to be up against energy problems for as long as we can see into the future. Which means we have to become less pampered, learn not to waste energy in the old sky-is-the-limit fashion, and be ready to face ever higher prices, especially for oil products. Recent events in Iran are just a sort of writing on the wall: on top of eventual scarcity, we have to think about world instability. Whether as a province or a sovereign Quebec, we must develop all of our abundant hydro resources, and diversify as much as possible away from too heavy a dependence on oil.

Are you prepared to pay international prices for crude oil and natural gas?

Eventually, I guess we'll all be paying international prices anyway. We're creeping up to them. I believe the main problem in the future is going to be not so much prices as security of supply.

While we are on the energy issue, could you describe your relations with Newfoundland with respect to the cost of Churchill Falls power?

In a nutshell, Newfoundland was very glad, in the sixties, to sign a contract with us which, by bringing in Hydro-Québec as co-developer and sole possible buyer, made the Churchill Falls project possible. And at the time, they were very happy to sign a contract which assured them of much needed revenue at what was then a respectable rate of return. Since the energy crisis of 1973-74, escalating energy prices have naturally made the contract look much less attractive. So by using a recall clause, they've brought their case to the courts. Consequently, the whole thing is now "sub judice". But may I remind you that, in similar circumstances, Quebec felt duty-bound, for more years than we like to remember, to live up to an old and ever increasingly unfavorable contract with Ontario?

Over the past few months both Quebec and the Federal government have produced balance sheets on Confederation. Which is correct?

Neither, I guess, if what you're looking for is a complete, crystal-clear assessment of costs and returns. There are always too many "grey areas" that you can't honestly evaluate. What remains indisputable, however, is that Quebec, along with the Maritimes generally, has been and still is getting the neck of the chicken as far as developing, job-creating Federal expenditures are concerned: something like

15% as an average, as against our normal 25% input in Ottawa's budget. Which keeps on maintaining that poisonous "division of labor" which is terribly rooted in tradition—development west of the Ottawa, dependence and hand-outs east.

How will you frame the referendum question? Are you seeking more than a mandate to negotiate or do you have something else in mind?

The question, whatever its final wording, will be based on those two joint perspectives we've been proposing since 1967–68: Sovereignty-Association. Since the two are coupled, and considering that both the transfer of powers required for sovereignty and the meeting of minds needed for association call for "reasoning together", we will be seeking a mandate to negotiate. But a yes vote will also mean that Quebecers have expressed a clear preference for our option and their belief in its feasibility. And I'd remind you that, while certainly not aggressive nor hostile towards anyone, our people would certainly not like their democratic decision to be denied or treated wrongly by others. And that's putting it mildly. . . .

Do you see a different negotiating strategy or position with the Federal government if the Federal Liberals are re-elected in 1979 and/or defeated?

About that we couldn't care less. Whether the sixteen-year-old Liberal government is reelected or defeated, is something of a superficial "epiphenomenon" as I put it in the book. What we want to get rid of for Quebec is not Liberal or Conservative administration, it's the stifling straight-jacket that the Federal system itself has become. All parties in Ottawa are part and parcel of that obsolete, mandarin-ridden regime. Once the system goes, Federal parties will automatically disappear from the Quebec scene, along with the crazy political schizophrenia they've kept us in for too long. So the sooner the better!